HEATHER LEFEBVRE

2000 Years of Faith, Fable, and Festivity

The History of Christmas

CF4•K

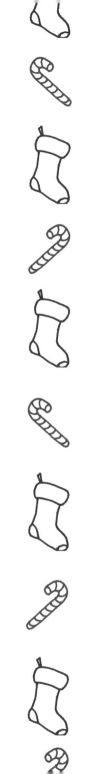

10 9 8 7 6 5 4 3 2
Copyright © 2019 Heather Winslow LeFebvre
Reprinted in 2020
ISBN: 978-1-5271-0334-4
Published by Christian Focus Publications,
Geanies House, Fearn, Tain, Ross-shire, IV20 1TW, U.K.
Printed and bound by Gutenberg, Malta

Illustrations by Laura C. Winslow
Cover Design by Creative Hoot

This book is the collaborative effort of a mother's artwork (Laura C. Winslow)
and a daughter's writing (Heather Winslow LeFebvre). It is born out of a lifetime
creating holiday memories and making art together, both in Laura's home when
Heather was a child and now in Heather's home where Grandma is a frequent
participant. We hope this book, the fruit of our holidays together, will inspire and
inform the readers' celebrations as well.

If you like history, you will love this Christmas book by Heather LeFebvre. If you don't like history, you should still read this one. Current events make more sense with knowledge of the past. The author gives a good review of western history by tracing the celebration of Christmas across the centuries, from the days of the Roman Empire to the 1950s in New York City. She does not take the traditional textbook approach to history. Instead she takes the reader into the homes and lives of ordinary people.

Russ Pulliam
Associate Editor, Indianapolis Star

Attractive, interesting and informative, this book is sure to liven your conversations this Christmas season. The timeline, activities, and discussion questions make it an excellent tool for homeschooling families. The text is Christ-focused and includes Luke's narrative of Jesus's birth and several short lists of suggested Bible readings. While the book is written for families who celebrate Christmas, it helps children to understand and respect the views of Christians who decide not to.

Simonetta Carr
Author of the Christian Biographies for Young Readers series

The History of Christmas is a wonderful journey through the traditions and ideas that have informed our celebration of Christ's birth. More than that, it's a study of people and events over the last 2,000 years that impacted the way we think about Christmas. Heather LeFebvre has written an engaging story of the way Christians have chosen to remember the Incarnation, complete with discussions, activities, and recipes for families to consider. With so much controversy over Christmas, it's important for families to know how Christmas really came to be–and to consider what it ought to become.

Danika Cooley
Children's author, Bible curriculum developer, and blogger at ThinkingKidsBlog.org

The hopes and fears of all the years are met in thee tonight. This warm and beautifully illustrated book captures something of the many years and many places touched by Jesus' coming to earth as our Lord and Saviour. It helps me see Christmas as something to be made, and made well. I'm looking forward to using its thoughtful questions and fun activities, as well as its practical suggestions and invitations, to help make my own Christmases more joyful and honoring to the Lord Jesus. Bring on Christmas!

Matthew Sleeman
Lecturer in New Testament and Greek, Oak Hill College, London

The History of Christmas is an excellent book that illustrates the reality behind the seasonal glitz and glitter of that time of year. Heather LeFebvre draws our attention to the truth of Christ's birth. Her focus on the message of Salvation makes this book an excellent addition to any family library. The activities and recipes are a fun, practical way to educate children about these festivities and the Christian faith.

Carine Mackenzie
Author of *The Bible Explorer* and *My First Book of Questions and Answers*

For my children:
Rachel, Drew,
James, David,
and Laura

Introducing Christmas

When we think of Christmas, our minds often turn to the decorations, the food, the frantic rushing about, the extended family we might see, and the presents exchanged in our holiday celebrations. We also think of Christ's birth in Bethlehem over two thousand years ago. Rarely do we reflect on the time between Christ's birth and the present, the time of medieval Christmas celebrations, or the scene in the Italian cave where St. Francis staged the first live Christmas nativity, or the years in Massachusetts when Christmas was illegal! We know the origin of Christmas, and our own, often hectic, experiences today, but we don't think about this holiday's long history.

The History of Christmas aims to take you on a journey from that night in Bethlehem when Christ was born, through Roman times and the Middle Ages, into Western Europe and the dawn of the Reformation, along into the Victorian era and the American West, and right up to our modern Christmas celebration. As you read, you'll discover the surprising twists and turns that Christmas celebrations have taken, and you'll recognize some of your own traditions and how they made their way to the twenty-first century.

Through all this history, you'll see the struggles that men and women went through trying to figure out how Christmas should, or should not, be celebrated. You'll see some of the problems that came with Christmas and the ideas people came up with to deal with them. You will also see how people attempted to use Christmas as a time to call attention to the birth and Incarnation of the Lord Jesus Christ and his love for mankind.

As you learn about the history of Christmas, it is my hope that you will be captivated by the beauty of history and the way that God works in our everyday lives year after year. I pray that thinking about Christmas will draw you closer to Christ and inspire you to show his love to those around you.

An Ordinary Day in Bethlehem
Bethlehem, c. 6 B.C.

A light wind rustled in the olive trees as new lambs, born just yesterday, jumped up and down and scuttled about on their wobbly legs. The sun shone brightly, warming the recently watered fields and drying the dew left overnight on the clumps of wild herbs. The mother sheep grazed contentedly, their safety assured by the presence of shepherds nearby. Sounds of carpenters beginning their day's labor, women talking in the street, and children yelling in play drifted out to the fields from the nearby town as the shepherds pulled leftover pieces of bread from their tunics to feed their hungry stomachs. It was an ordinary day in Bethlehem, but it was destined to be remembered forever as the first Christmas.

It was about 6 B.C in Bethlehem, a small town just six miles (10 km) south of Jerusalem. This town had once been the home of Israel's most famous king: David. On these fertile, hillside pastures, David had shepherded his father's flocks. Inside the town, David had been anointed king by the prophet Samuel. In nearby Jerusalem, David had been promised by God that one of his heirs would one day be born the promised Messiah. Nearly a thousand years had passed since that promise. Only the most devout Jews still looked for the fulfillment of that long-ago promise. Brutal and powerful Rome had swept across the country and made it her own. A puppet king had been put in place: a selfish and evil man named Herod, a Jewish imposter whose lineage couldn't be further from David's royal line.

Bethlehem was busier than usual on this day. Its small population of 300 was swelling as families arrived from distant places to be registered in a government-mandated census. Every house had extra guests. The streets were filled with children making new friends with cousins they had never met, darting between buildings in hopes of getting out to the fields to play before their mothers called them home to work. Men talked in hushed tones about the Roman rule that sat like a heavy burden on their backs. The lines at the well were longer, but the women didn't seem to mind the extra moments to hear the latest bits of news from distant villages. The older women listed off the names of families that had moved from Bethlehem over the years, making a mental list of who might yet turn up for the Roman census. The town was full to bursting already. If anyone else came, who knows where they would stay?

Nine months earlier a young woman, Mary, had been calmly going about her housework when she had heard the startling words, "Greetings, O favored one, the Lord is with you!" Mary was well-schooled in the Hebrew scriptures and knew this was no ordinary greeting, and no ordinary messenger. The angel told her not to be afraid, explaining that the Holy Spirit would cause a child to be born to Mary even though she was not yet married to her fiancé, Joseph. Mary believed the words of the angel and soon found herself miraculously pregnant.

When word came to Joseph that Mary was pregnant, what could he think but that she had been unfaithful to him. Joseph was kind and God-fearing. He didn't want to put Mary through a shameful public breaking of their engagement. Joseph wondered if he could work this out quietly without many people knowing. However, before Joseph could break the engagement, he had a dream. An angel, a messenger from heaven, explained to Joseph that Mary was carrying a baby given to her by God. Joseph was not to be afraid to wed Mary, and the baby was to be named Jesus. Joseph, like Mary, believed the words of the angel and Mary and Joseph got married.

Joseph and Mary were now on the way to Bethlehem to participate in the required census. The long week of walking through the hilly terrain would tire any fit person, but it would be especially difficult on young Mary in her pregnant condition. Joseph knew the names of relatives with whom they might be able to find room when they arrived in Bethlehem. Surely between them, there would be a place for Mary to lie down.

It was more difficult to find a lodging place than one might expect, even with plenty of relatives in town. It seemed that Bethlehem was already filled to capacity for the census. Too many people had arrived before Mary and Joseph. Houses were filled to bursting with aunts, uncles, cousins, and siblings.

Eventually someone took pity on Joseph and Mary and found room for them, most likely in an already overcrowded home. In those days, people and animals shared the same housing space. The first floor of each home would be partitioned off for people on one side and animals on the other. The dividing wall would hold a feeding trough, or manger.

And so it was that Mary gave birth to her baby. They named him Jesus as the angel had instructed. The only safe place to put baby Jesus was the long feed trough, possibly stained and matted with the remnants of years of animal feed. The Prince of Peace, King of Kings, and Savior of men was sleeping in a humble manger.

With Jesus resting safely in the feed trough, Mary might have sipped curdled sheep's milk and torn bites from a barley loaf. Perhaps later she might eat some lentil stew. No doubt the weariness of birthing a baby caused her to wish for rest and sleep.

Outside the village, shepherds gathered around a fire. The warm air of the spring day would have dissipated into near-freezing when the sun set. The men possibly exchanged news of ewes that had given birth, or the number of lambs born. Barley loaves would have been shared, toasted almonds passed around, sheep curds slurped. Theirs was a simple life and it was to these simple folk that the angel of the Lord appeared in heavenly glory on that dark and cold night. Fear like they had never known gripped their hearts. Their eyes likely widened in amazement and their hands trembled as the angel urged them not to fear. There was good news for these shepherds tonight. Good news of great joy! The age-old promise of a Savior had been fulfilled today in the town of Bethlehem after so many years of waiting. This Savior could be found in the town, lying in a feeding trough. Suddenly, the angel was joined by a huge choir of angels giving praise to God and saying, "Glory to God in the highest, and on earth peace among those with whom he is pleased!"

17

The shepherds followed the angel's instruction and hurried into the town to check every feeding trough until they found one with a baby lying in it! Perhaps they smiled at the thought: a feeding trough, of all places for a Savior to be born! However, there was the baby, and there were his parents just as the angel had said. The shepherds could hardly contain their joy and wonder, calling to the people nearby to hear their story, the story of the angels in the sky and the baby in the feeding trough.

One day a group of travelers (called a caravan) made its way south from Jerusalem, winding through the hills and then the narrow streets of Bethlehem. This entourage might have contained camels, donkeys, and servants, as well as the foreign men of great importance and obvious wealth that Matthew's Gospel records. The caravan was following a star that eventually rested over the house where Jesus was staying. Finding a child inside the house, the foreign men fell at his feet and worshiped. This was the King of the Jews they had traveled all the way from their home in Mesopotamia to see. This was the king whose birth had been foretold in the heavens and whose location had been revealed to them by the traveling star. This was the king worthy to receive the gifts they had brought: gold, frankincense, and myrrh.

It had been wicked and jealous King Herod who had helped the learned men from the east find Bethlehem. This treacherous king had wanted them to return and report to him the exact location of this newly born king. Herod claimed he wanted to worship this baby. In truth,

 18

Herod wanted to kill the child and snuff out any possible rival for his throne.

It was another dream that intervened and warned the wise men not to return to Herod. Instead, they packed up their caravan and headed back to Mesopotamia by a different route, leaving Herod furious at being outwitted and uninformed. In his wrath, he ordered the killing of all male children two years old and under in the region of Bethlehem. By the time Herod's soldiers reached Bethlehem, Joseph, Mary, and Jesus were long gone. Joseph had received a dream as well. This dream warned that Herod was seeking the death of Jesus and gave instructions for the family to flee to Egypt.

And so the story of the birth of Christ comes to an end. Mary remembered these events and thought upon them in her heart. Most likely no one else thought much about Jesus' birthday, and he most certainly would not have had any sort of birthday party or birthday celebration during his life. Birthdays were not a big deal in Bible times, and few people could read or write or have the ability to record a specific date. No one was concerned about when Jesus was born. Everyone was focused on who Jesus was and what he had come to do. It would be many years before anyone would begin to wonder about when it was that Christ was born.

Suggested Scriptures

Luke 2:1-21; Matthew 1:18-2:18

Discussion Questions

- Are you surprised that King Jesus was born in such humble conditions?

- Why is it important that Jesus lived on this earth just like you: as a baby, then as a child and teenager, and finally as an adult?

- How would the characters in the story have felt God's love for them?

- Do you enjoy having guests at your house? How would it have felt in the house where Jesus was born?

- Would you miss celebrating your birthday if you lived in the first century?

- How would you have felt if you were one of the shepherds the angels appeared to?

- What is your favorite part of the Christmas story?

 20

Enjoy a Shepherd's Meal

Shepherds in Israel lived a humble existence, caring for sheep and goats. Their food was simple: bread, cheese, nuts, fruits, and perhaps a lentil stew. Create a simple "Shepherd's Meal" and pretend you are living in first century Judea. Gather crusy bread, cheese, toasted almonds, dried dates, figs, or raisins to enjoy alongside this Savoury Lentil Soup. As you bite the crusty bread or taste the savory soup, think about how those shepherds felt to be the first to worship the Messiah.

Savory Lentil Soup

Ingredients:

- 4 tbsp./60ml olive oil
- 1 large onion, diced
- 2 large carrots, peeled and diced
- 2 stalks celery, chopped
- 4 cloves garlic, minced
- 1 tsp. ground cumin
- 1 tsp. curry powder
- 8 cups/2 liters chicken or vegetable stock

- 14.5 oz can diced tomatoes/400g tin chopped tomatoes
- 1 ½ cups/284g red lentils, rinsed
- 2 tbsp./30ml lemon juice
- chopped parsley to serve

Method:

Heat olive oil in a large pot. Sauté onion, carrots, and celery over medium heat until onion begins to soften, 5-8 minutes.

Add minced garlic, cumin, and curry powder, frying until fragrant, about one minute.

Pour in the stock, tomatoes with any juice, and rinsed lentils. Bring to the boil. Simmer for 30 minutes until the lentils are soft.

Stir in the lemon juice and adjust seasoning to taste.

Serve with a garnish of chopped parsley.

Serves 4-6.

A Date for Christ's Nativity
Constantinople, Fourth Century A.D.

The days were short, the weather on the dreary side, the temperatures a chilly 40-50°F (4.5-10°C). What Rome lacked in good weather, it made up for in feasting and merriment. Crowds lined the streets dressed in colorful robes, their spirits soaring from being let out of work and school for a holiday. Women carried home bundles of candles, ready to give as gifts to friends and relatives. Children ran wild in the streets. Slaves changed places with their masters and gave orders to their superiors. Food and wine were abundant. Wreaths and greenery decorated the houses. Extravagance, foolishness, and inappropriate behavior were expected. This was known as the best time of the year.

It might sound like a Christmas celebration, but it was not. This was the annual feast of Saturnalia, celebrating the god of agriculture and time. For hundreds of years, the feast to Saturn had been celebrated by Romans who loved the chance to stop work and indulge themselves. Feasts containing all types of delicious breads, cheeses, baked and roasted meats, dried fruit, honey cakes, and spiced and honeyed wine were organized. Raucous singing in the streets took place. For seven days, from December 17 to 23, the citizens of the Roman Empire forgot their daily troubles and drowned their woes with revelry. Having such a feast to look forward to helped to pass the dull and dreary winter months.

Saturnalia wasn't the only December feast the Romans celebrated. The winter solstice occurred on December 25 when they celebrated "Dies Natalis Solis Invicti," or the birthday of Sol, the Unconquered Sun. This god was so important to the Romans that he appeared on their coins for many years and was named as the principal patron of the empire.

Living among all the devoted worshipers of Saturn and the sun god, Sol, was a group of people known as Christians. These followers of the teachings of Jesus Christ had grown in number from several hundred to several million by the fourth century. After Jesus' ascension to heaven around A.D. 30, the Christians organized themselves into what became known as the early church. These men and women believed Christ's return to earth was going to be very soon. With their thoughts focused on the possibility of this world coming quickly to an end, they never thought about commemorating Christ's birthday or even taking note of when it was that Christ was born. Birthdays in the Bible were only ever noted for characters portrayed as harmful to God's people: Pharaoh and King Herod. Commemorating a birthday was a pagan practice and of no interest to those early followers of Christ.

Time marched forward and Christ did not return as soon as the early Christians had thought. Instead

of being rescued quickly from this earth, they found themselves the focus of a brutal and deadly persecution. This persecution swept the Roman Empire and left many Christians martyred for their faith. As more and more beloved and honored men and women died, the Christians started to record the martyrs' dates of death to remember these anniversaries with prayer or worship services. Over time, a list of the death dates of martyrs was collected.

Around the same time that the dates of martyrs' deaths began to be written down, other records show that Christians were remembering the baptism of Christ, the beginning of his ministry, and even his birth with a feast they named Epiphany (meaning manifestation) and celebrated on January 6. This was an addition to the feast of Christ's resurrection, Pascha, which they already celebrated and which we know today as Easter.

The date for Pascha was easy to determine because Christ had died and risen again during the Jewish Passover feast. The date for the Passover feast was based on the phases of the moon and held in the spring of each year. By the early fourth century, the Church had a yearly calendar that included celebrations for Christ's death and resurrection (Pascha), Christ's manifestation to men (Epiphany), and the death dates of many Christian martyrs.

In A.D. 313, an unimaginable thing happened: the Roman Emperor, Constantine, appeared to convert to Christianity and published the Edict of Milan, giving religious freedom to Christians. Suddenly, it was not only legal to worship the Christian God, it was actually even encouraged! Christians came out of hiding. Churches could be built in the open. Large crowds could gather in public for worship. Everything was different.

It was during Constantine's reign that December 25 began to be associated with the birth of Christ. In A.D. 345, Julian, the leader of churches in Rome, declared December 25 to be the birthday of Christ and a separate celebration from the Epiphany celebration on January 6. No one knows how the December 25 date was decided upon. Some scholars guess that turning the birthday of the Unconquered Sun into the birthday of the true Son of God

seemed like a natural way to help the pagan Romans embrace the newly endorsed Christian religion. It certainly was convenient. Other scholars trace the December 25 date from the legend of Christ's death being on the same date as that of his conception, using March 25 for both dates and counting forward nine months for a December 25 birthday. The Eastern church would claim Christ's death and conception to be on April 9 and thus count forward to the January 6 date.

Emperor Constantine split the Roman Empire into two parts: the Western Roman Empire which was governed out of Rome, and the Eastern Roman Empire which was governed out of a new city which Constantine named Constantinople. Not only was the political Empire split in half, but the Christian Church found itself divided in two. Christians in the West followed what would soon become known as the Roman Catholic Church and Christians in the East followed the traditions of what would become the Eastern Orthodox Church. These two groups had many similarities, but there were some differences. One of those differences was the date for Christ's birth.

25

***

Light streamed through the side windows of the church and fell on the crowd of people gathered to worship in Constantinople, the new capital of the Roman Empire. A man in a long robe stood at the front, leading the congregation through the order of service. This gathering no longer needed to be held in secret, thanks to the end of persecution and the acceptance of Christianity as an approved religion of the Roman Empire.

"My ears resound to the Shepherd's song," rang the words from the front. "The Angels sing. The Archangels blend their voice in harmony. The Cherubim hymn their joyful praise. The Seraphim exalt His glory." The words of the sermon fell like gold dust on the heads of the worshipers

crowded into the Church of Holy Wisdom. "All join to praise this holy feast, beholding the Godhead here on earth, and man in heaven. He who is above, now for our redemption dwells here below; and he that was lowly is by divine mercy raised."

John Chrysostom, the newly appointed Archbishop of Constantinople, was delivering his nativity sermon. With well-chosen words and deep emotion, he was urging his congregation to take notice of the upcoming anniversary of the birth of Christ. He begged them to prepare for this day with thoughtful confession of sin and examination of their behavior. The sermon continued on, as Chrysostom recounted the events of that first nativity: the Incarnation of God in the form of a baby, the virgin mother, the birthplace in Bethlehem, the angels' visit to the shepherds, the gifts of the wise men. His pastor's heart longed for the congregation to comprehend the miracle of Christ's birth and the spiritual importance it still held for them today. He called them to celebrate on December 25, personally convinced this was actually the date of Christ's birth.

Chrysostom was not imagining a feast day for Christ's birth, filled with pagan revelry or over-indulgence or excessive waste of money. He envisioned a church feast day commemorated by worship, repentance, and devotion. Over and over again he emphasized temperance and virtue, self-examination and repentance. He chided the congregation for spending excess money on fancy clothes and indulgent feasts, when they ought to be concerned about their spiritual health.

In the century that followed Constantine and Chyrsostom, the December 25 celebration of Christ's nativity became universally celebrated throughout the eastern and western empire. As the Roman Empire fell apart and Christian missionaries were sent to lands far, far away, they took the church calendar, and thus the celebration of Christ's nativity, with them.

Suggested Reading

Acts 1:6-11; 2:42-47; Matthew 10:16-23

Discussion Questions

- What do you think it would have been like to be a Christian during the Roman persecution?

- If you were a Christian in Roman times, how would you explain to your friends that you didn't celebrate the feast of Saturnalia?

- Do you see any similarities between the celebration of Saturnalia and Christmas today?

- How would you have felt when the Roman Emperor converted to Christianity?

- Does your family keep a list of birthdays of relatives and close friends?

- Do you think it is important to know the exact date of Christ's birth?

- What was John Chrysostom so concerned that his congregation do, in order to remember Christ's birth?

Bake a Batch of Cookies

The Romans loved honey cookies. They took the idea from the Egyptians and Greeks, adding their own touch as the years went on. Refined sugar was not available, so they used honey instead as a sweetener. When you take a bite of these delicious cookies, imagine what it must have felt like to be a persecuted Christian in a pagan, Roman culture. Thank God for the freedoms you enjoy today, and pray for Christians who suffer persecution in other countries.

Roman Honey-Sesame Cookies

Ingredients:
- 2 ½ cups/350g all-purpose flour
- 1 tsp. baking powder
- ¼ tsp. salt
- ⅛ tsp. (pinch) baking soda
- ½ cup/113g butter, softened
- ½ cup/118ml clear honey
- 2 eggs
- ½ cup/50g sesame seeds
- 4 tbsp./56g melted butter

Method:

Preheat oven to 350F/ 180C/160C Fan. In a bowl, combine the flour, baking powder, salt, and baking soda. Use a whisk to thoroughly mix the dry ingredients together. Set aside.

In the bowl of a stand mixer, beat the softened butter and honey together. Add the eggs and beat until well-combined. Gradually mix in the dry ingredients. Chill the dough for one hour or until firm.

Roll the chilled dough into balls approximately 1-inch/2.5cm in size. Place on a greased cookie sheet. Bake for approximately 12 minutes. Watch for over-browning as honey burns faster than granulated sugar. Cool cookies on a wire rack, then brush the tops with melted butter and immediately dip in sesame seeds. Makes about 25.

Boniface Spreads Christianity
Germany, Winter A.D. 725

A solemn crowd gathered under towering trees deep in a German forest. There was little light, and the winter air chilled the group clad in their worn linen tunics and woolen capes. A hush had fallen on the people, and their attention was focused on the enormous oak tree standing in the middle of the grove. It was the sacred Oak of Thor, the god of thunder, storms, strength, and fertility. The oak was so large, and its branches so far-reaching, that its years could be numbered in the hundreds.

The people had left their one-room thatched homes back in the village to journey into the forest. They were mindful that crops had not been good in recent years, and there had been little success in defending their lands from invaders. It was midwinter and the feast of Yule was upon them. It was supposed to be one of the happiest times of the year, full of feasting, merriment, and well-wishing. They'd taken care to decorate their homes with evergreens, holly, and mistletoe, and searched the wooded areas for giant Yule logs which could smolder for twelve days on their hearths. Everyone was looking forward to the promise of meat for the celebration, and of extra portions of their usual bread, vegetables, and ale.

Despite the festive time of year, they felt the displeasure of Thor and his demand for a sacrifice, a very costly sacrifice. Fear gripped the hearts of those in the forest, and every mother trembled at the thought of their child being chosen as the sacrifice to appease Thor.

The sound of snapping twigs and brush broke the heavy silence. Eyes darted to the edge of the glade as the bushes parted and a man in a long robe, a rope around his waist, and his head shaved on the top came into view. He carried an axe in his right hand and a staff in the left as he marched purposefully toward the oak. "Friends," he cried. "I tell you again, you have placed your hope in a false god, a pagan deity who has no power to help you. This god, Thor, whom you worship, is no god at all. And there is no need for you to sacrifice to him. Don't let your children be taken. Believe in the Lord Jesus Christ who was sacrificed once and for all on your behalf. His death atoned for your sins and his resurrection proves his sacrifice was accepted."

The people stood in shocked silence as the man, whom they knew by the name of Boniface, approached the Oak. Boniface raised the axe in his hand and called out, "I will show you that Thor is powerless to help you." Boniface swung the axe behind his head and brought it crashing into the side of the tree. A collective gasp could be heard in the crowd, yet no one moved to stop the man. "If Thor is a real

god, let him stop me from cutting down this tree," continued Boniface as he pulled the axe back to swing again. At that moment, a mighty wind rushed through the glade. An ear-piercing crack was heard as the Oak of Thor crashed into the forest and fell with an earth-shaking thud to the ground. As it landed, the mighty oak split into four pieces and lay silent.

The people looked up through the open space to the sky. They saw no storm, they heard no thunder. Was the message Boniface preached to them true? Was it possible Thor was a false god, unable to help them? Perhaps the God of the Bible was the true God.

***

Boniface, born "Winfrid" sometime around A.D. 680 in Devonshire, England, became known as the Apostle to the Germans. He grew up in England at a time when the worship traditions of the English Church were slowly being harmonized to match the worship traditions of the churches in Italy and other parts of southern Europe. Christianity had come to Britain very quickly because of the Roman occupation in the first and second centuries. After the breakdown of the Roman Empire, the churches in England had to survive on their own without oversight from Rome. They developed their own traditions for worship services and festivals, specifically their own system for determining the date of Easter, and their own style of shaving the heads of their monks. The work of St. Patrick in Ireland and St. Columba in Scotland helped the churches to spread and grow. This area of the Christian Church became known as the Celtic Church.

Shortly before Boniface was born, a missionary by the name of Augustine was sent to England by the Roman pope. His job was to preach the gospel, strengthen the struggling churches, and help organize the churches to be more consistent with the Roman churches. By the time Boniface was born, there was a great allegiance to the pope in Rome as the head of all the churches, including those in England. This meant that the church calendar the Romans were following eventually became the church calendar in England. The celebration of Easter dominated the calendar as the most important Christian feast of the year. In fact, Easter was known as the beginning of the church year.

We also know that at the end of the sixth century, Pope Gregory the Great authorized three masses, or church services, to be celebrated for Christ's nativity on December 25. This church calendar, which also included feasts for several of the apostles, and days to remember many of the martyrs, was the church calendar Boniface grew up with and the one he took with him when he decided to venture out as a missionary to the European continent.

It was a turbulent time in Europe. There was no Roman Emperor on the throne anymore. Barbarian tribes flowed through Europe, conquering and being conquered. Pagan practices were common: human sacrifice, animal sacrifice, superstition, witchcraft. Christianity had reached some corners of Europe, but without regular teaching and instruction these places tended to revert back to paganism once the Christian missionary died.

Boniface felt a great call to preach the gospel in foreign lands. Having been raised as a monk and having received a solid education in the faith, he was ready to share this faith with others. In A.D. 719, Boniface was commissioned by Pope

Gregory II to preach the gospel in northern Europe, specifically in the area which is now Germany. For the next thirty-five years, Boniface slowly and methodically traveled around northern Europe preaching the gospel, organizing monasteries and nunneries, building churches, and revitalizing any faint glimmer of Christianity that remained. His biggest challenge was convincing the people to give up their pagan practices. Often it came down to showing the people that their god had no power. Cutting down the Oak of Thor helped the people understand that there was no true power behind this pagan deity.

Once an ethnic group converted to Christianity, there was a question of what to do about their traditions, ceremonies, and rituals which were ingrained in them from childhood and had become a part of their way of life. No one wanted to give up celebrations that helped make winter more bearable. It seemed to the pope that the best thing would be to Christianize these practices to make it easier for former pagans to transition to a Christian life. Over time, this meant that many of the midwinter symbols and practices such as holly, mistletoe, caroling, and Yule logs were associated with the birth of Christ rather than the celebration of a midwinter solstice or a pagan fertility god.

The work of Boniface was so monumental that it can be considered as one of the greatest developments of eighth-century Europe. The Christianization of Germany and the unification of the churches with Rome became a stabilizing influence that enabled Europe to eventually move out of the Dark Ages and into a time of growth and development.

Boniface ended his many years of mission work with a final mission to Frisia, which is now the Netherlands. His mission was fruitful and there were many baptized and called out for confirmation. One day, Boniface and his group were attacked by armed robbers who killed Boniface, hoping to steal valuable goods from him. The robbers found only books, and no treasure, and Europe lost one of its most devoted missionaries. Boniface was no more, but the men and women converted through him passed their faith on to future generations, and lands that had once been pagan became known as Christian lands. As the centuries went by, the celebration of Christ's nativity became more widely known and more universally celebrated because of the work of missionaries like Boniface.

Suggested Reading

Matthew 28:18-20; Romans 10:11-15

Discussion Questions

- Do you think it was hard for Boniface to leave his homeland to be a missionary?
- Was there another way for Europe to hear the gospel without missionaries being sent?
- Do you think Pope Gregory had a good idea when he asked that pagan traditions be turned into Christian traditions?
- Do you recognize any of the Yule decorations or traditions as part of your Christmas today?
- Do you think it is helpful to have a midwinter feast to look forward to when it is so dark and cold?
- Did bringing Christianity to pagan Europe cause it to be a more peaceful place?
- How can you be a missionary in your own home town?

Bite Into an Edible Tree Trunk

Legend tells us that it was the felling of the great Oak of Thor that played a part in persuading the Frankish people to abandon their pagan gods and put their trust in Christ. Bake a batch of Oak Log Cookies and think about the courage and faith Boniface had to leave his homeland in England and become a missionary in Germany. How would you feel about becoming a missionary?

Oak Log Cookies

Ingredients:
- 1 cup/227g butter, softened
- ¾ cup/150g brown sugar
- 2 tbsp. orange juice
- zest of one orange
- 2 ½ cups/350g all-purpose flour
- ¼ tsp. salt
- 1 cup/4 oz finely chopped hazelnuts or pecans
- 2 tbsp. water

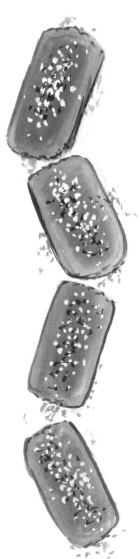

Method:

Preheat oven to 350F/180C/160C Fan.

In the bowl of a stand mixer, cream the butter and brown sugar together. Beat in the orange juice and zest.

In a separate bowl, mix together the flour and salt. Add the flour mixture to the butter mixture and gently mix until a dough forms.

On a floured surface, roll out portions of dough into long ropes about ½ inch/1.25cm thick.

Cut sections of the rope into 2-inch/5cm logs. Brush the tops of the cookie logs with water and dip into the chopped nuts.

Place on a greased or parchment paper lined cookie sheet. Bake cookies for approximately 12 minutes until light brown.

Place on wire racks to cool. Makes about 42 cookies.

Christmas Gets a Name
London, Christmas Day A.D. 1066

Two boys peered out from behind the long row of soldiers lining the narrow London street. Just minutes before, a large procession had passed on the way to the new abbey at St. Peter's Monastery.

"Did you see him, Geoffrey?" asked the boy with a shock of blond hair and a dirt-stained tunic. "Yes, yes, Simon, I did!" Geoffrey whispered excitedly. "It's something new having a Norman to be our king," Simon continued. "Do you think there will be trouble?" Geoffrey looked at Simon as if he had never considered that. "I hope not," he replied. "Come on, let's get closer to the abbey."

The boys struggled through the crowds of onlookers who were held in place by the rows of soldiers and horses. "Were you up early for mass this morning?" Simon asked when they found a place to stand near the abbey's entrance. "It was Shepherd's Mass at dawn for us," Geoffrey said yawning. "And that was after attending the Angel's Mass at midnight. I'm sure my mother will be looking for me for the mid-day mass as well," he continued, "but with the hundreds of churches in London, maybe I'll just duck into whichever church is closest."

"Won't you be rewarded with plenty of food at your table later today?" asked Simon with a wistful look in his eyes, thinking about how his mother had made him fast yesterday for Christmas Eve. "My mother has a large joint of meat on the fire, and my father was collecting extra jugs of ale for tonight," Simon rattled on, "We even have spices and dried fruit to add to the ale to make wassail," his voice betrayed anticipation.

"Yes, I'm eager for the food," admitted Geoffrey, "and the warmth of the huge Yule log we pulled in from the forest yesterday. Why, I'm sure it will burn

39

for a month, not just the twelve days of Christmas."

"Did your mother make you gather holly and ivy for decorating?" asked Geoffrey as they passed another row of long, wooden houses on their way to St. Peter's Monastery. Simon laughed as he replied, "I escaped that one because I have so many sisters. My mother is superstitious. She wants plenty of greenery decorating our house to scare away the evil spirits that roam around at this dark time of year. I know the church doesn't approve of the sacred mistletoe, but mother found some growing on a tree in the middle of the woods outside the city walls and persuaded my dad to let her have it." Geoffrey broke in, "Well, my father wastes all the delicious wassail by pouring it out on the bottom of the apple trees in my grandfather's orchard on the Twelfth Night. He says it will make the crops fruitful."

"Look!" interrupted Simon as they approached the abbey at St. Peter's, "There goes William the Conqueror into the abbey!" Geoffrey craned his neck to see the group of men clad in tunics and mantles, with a red-haired man at the center. "Imagine spending your Christmas

like this," scoffed Geoffrey. "If I was king, I'd want to be in the palace enjoying the feast of boar's head, mince pies, roasted chicken and pigeon, plum porridge, and all the wassail I could drink." Geoffrey's eyes took on a far away look just thinking about all that food. "Oh, he'll have that no doubt," replied Simon, "and plenty more."

The boys settled down to wait as the last of William's retinue entered the abbey and the knights took up their watch on the outside of the building. Last year, on December 28, Holy Innocent's Day, the newly expanded church was consecrated by King Edward the Confessor.

But a week later Edward was dead. The boys remembered the coronation of Harold that soon followed in this same abbey. "I wish I could have been at the Battle of Hastings," Geoffrey blurted out. "Imagine the excitement of the battle, and then the death of King Harold and the defeat of the Anglo-Saxons by William and his Norman army." Simon rolled his eyes. "It was better you were safely here in London."

***

The year was 1066 during the time of the European Middle Ages. England had just been conquered by William of Normandy at the Battle of Hastings. William chose Christmas Day for his London coronation, perhaps because Christmas was the beginning of the Anglo-Saxon year and had become the most popular religious celebration in all of Europe. Perhaps William wanted to identify himself with Charlemagne, King of the Franks, who had been crowned Holy Roman Emperor on Christmas Day, A.D. 800. Whatever reason, the celebration of Jesus' nativity on December 25 was now rooted deeply in European culture, and by 1038 was being called "Cristes Maesse" in Old English, meaning "Christ's Mass." (A mass is what the Roman Church called a worship service

that included communion.) After 1000 years, the celebration of the birth of Christ finally had a name: Christmas.

The Roman Catholic Church, which was the only kind of church in Western Europe, had developed an intricate set of celebrations for this Christmas season. St. Martin's Day on November 11 ushered in the beginning of a time called Advent and the start of the nativity season. Advent's original purpose was to be a period of fasting and preparation, similar to Lent, leading up to the great feast of Christmas.

St. Thomas' Day was celebrated on December 21, also the day of the winter solstice. This "day of darkness" was commemorated by Thomas because he was the disciple to remain in the "darkness of unbelief" for the longest time. Christmas Eve and Christmas Day followed on December 24 and 25. St. Stephen's Day, commemorating the first martyr, came the day after Christmas on December 26 and the ominous Holy Innocent's Day, on December 28, marked the killing of the Bethlehem infants by wicked King Herod. January 6 brought Epiphany and concluded the twelve days of Christmas begun on December 25. The entire season came to a final end on February 2 with Candlemas, the celebration of Mary's purification and Jesus' presentation in the temple. Such a series of holidays may sound exhausting to our modern ears, but this lengthy time of feasting and revelry, religious devotion and pageantry, was the best medicine a medieval person knew for fighting the darkness and depression of a cold European winter.

Christmas in Medieval England was an intricate collage of traditional pagan practices and church rituals. Christmas had become a tug-of-war between the Church, which wanted to keep Christ at the center of life and worship, and the people, who wanted to have a fun time at the end of a long, hard year. Many Christmas practices were steeped in superstition and were hard for the uneducated peasants to give up. The peasants had no deep understanding of why they should discontinue a ritual that had been practiced for generations.

Gradually the Church gave new meanings to the pagan traditions. The Yule log eventually came to represent a fire that burned to keep the Christ child warm, rather than a fire kept burning to ensure the sun's return to the earth. The evergreen holly with its red berries had been used to provide protection from thunderstorms and the power of witches, but gradually came to represent the eternal life of Christ and his blood shed on the cross.

Christmas celebrations were different for different groups of people. Monks in a monastery might keep Advent very strictly with all the rules for fasting carefully observed, anticipating extra religious services added to their daily routine to celebrate Christ's birth. The monks might receive gifts of extra food and drink from local benefactors on Christmas Eve to make their Christmas meal into a feast.

A commoner in England might not want to observe the fasting of Advent as carefully as the monks. Life in the Middle Ages meant that there wasn't enough money for extra food or entertainment leading up to Christmas. Families might try to set aside extra ale for the twelve days of Christmas — the time period between Christmas and Epiphany. A housewife might save the largest joint of meat from a recent butchering for the Christmas feast. If she could afford to, she might purchase spices and dried fruit to make wassail, a spiced alcoholic drink enjoyed at this season.

The whole country tried to keep work to a minimum during the twelve days of Christmas so time could be spent indulging in gambling, drinking, and merriment with one's neighbors. The bad weather at this time of year often guaranteed safety from enemies and allowed the commoners freedom from concern about invaders. Gifts did not play a large role in the actual Christmas celebrations. If gifts were given at all, they would be to children on December 6, the feast of St. Nicholas, or on January 1, New Year's Day.

For the wealthy, Christmas was much grander. Money was spent on extra food, ale, and entertainment. Great houses and castles would be decked with holly. Incredible amounts of food would be consumed including a great boar's head paraded into the feast with music and an array of other dishes. Sweet dishes were not yet popular, but dried fruits and spices were added to savory dishes. The mince pie, filled with chopped up, left-over meat, suet, and spices, with dried fruit to add sweetness, was in its early stages of development as a food associated with Christmas. Wealthy households could afford to hire a minstrel for musical and humorous entertainment.

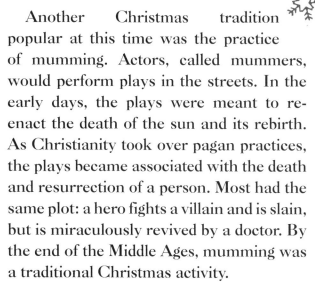

Another Christmas tradition popular at this time was the practice of mumming. Actors, called mummers, would perform plays in the streets. In the early days, the plays were meant to re-enact the death of the sun and its rebirth. As Christianity took over pagan practices, the plays became associated with the death and resurrection of a person. Most had the same plot: a hero fights a villain and is slain, but is miraculously revived by a doctor. By the end of the Middle Ages, mumming was a traditional Christmas activity.

William the Conqueror's reign heralded the beginning of Norman England, a time period that would carry England from the depths of the Dark Ages into the light of the Renaissance and Reformation. Europe would slowly transform into a continent dotted with bustling cities, growing centers of learning, and a more clearly defined idea of what was pagan and what was Christian.

As the Middle Ages came to a close, the Christmas season had become a rich and cultured time of year. Pagan practices had melted into Christian tradition and no one remembered where one ended and the other began.

Suggested Reading

Isaiah 60:1-3; Isaiah 9:1-7

Discussion Questions

- Would you choose Christmas Day for your coronation if you were a king or queen? Why or why not?

- If you lived in Medieval England, how would you celebrate Christmas?

- Would you prefer to be a monk, a commoner, or a wealthy landowner?

- Would you have liked the original mince pies with leftover meats and no sugar?

- How did Christianity change the pagan winter celebrations with their decorations and traditions?

- There were no Christmas gifts in Medieval times. Would you find that a difficult change?

- Can you find similarities between Christmas today and Christmas in Medieval England?

24 Ways to do a Medieval Christmas

1. Go to church
2. Decorate your home with fresh evergreens, ivy, and holly
3. Hang up some mistletoe
4. Make non-alcoholic wassail to drink
5. Burn a Yule log in your fireplace (or make a Yule log cake!)
6. Eat dinner by candlelight
7. Celebrate Christmas for twelve days
8. Gather with friends to sing carols
9. Put on a Christmas play
10. Have a game of tug-of-war
11. Play a game of chess
12. Create a "Gingerbread Castle"
13. Try having venison, rabbit, duck, or goose for dinner
14. Exchange gifts on New Year's Day rather than Christmas
15. Put together food baskets to give as gifts
16. Flavor your food with pepper, ginger, cloves, or nutmeg
17. Try a medieval Christmas pudding by stirring dried fruit, cinnamon, and nutmeg into a pot of thick oatmeal
18. Try making mince pies with fruit AND meat
19. Serve oranges, figs, and dates for dessert
20. Eat a meat pie
21. Serve a meal on slices of bread (trenchers) rather than plates
22. Practice juggling and entertain your family at dinner
23. Eat dinner with your fingers
24. Serve your meal in courses and announce each one with a trumpet sound

St. Francis and the Live Nativity
Italy, Christmas Eve A.D. 1223

It was Christmas Eve in Greccio, Italy, a tiny hill town about sixty miles north of Rome. Just past mid-afternoon the sun had fallen on the olive groves and vineyards surrounding the village. The damp, cold weather lay on the countryside like a frozen blanket. Greccio's inhabitants were huddled together in their cramped, wooden homes, partaking of the traditional Christmas Eve meatless dinner and awaiting the first mass of Christmas at the midnight hour. Unexpectedly, the sound of singing floated into the town, growing louder by the minute as the words to Psalm 98 became clear: "Sing to the LORD a new song, for he has done marvelous things!"

People jumped up and ran to their doors, peering out into the darkness to see who it could be. Friars, in the long, rough, woolen robes which such men wore, held torches and candles as they continued singing, "The LORD has made known his salvation."

A young boy ran up to the houses, calling and shouting as he passed, "Come up the mountain. Come to hear Francesco speak." Word spread that Francesco was calling for the townspeople. Men, women, and children, holding their own smoking torches and bundled against the cold, slowly gathered on the village path. The crowd joined the friars in the singing as they began to march into the oak forest. The people knew without being told that they were heading up toward the hermitage — the tiny, cramped cell in the hillside where Francesco, their beloved monk from Assisi, stayed when he visited.

The torches lit the way as the forest closed in on the curious group. No one knew what to expect, but everyone loved Francesco and his passionate commitment to Christ Jesus. With careful footsteps and joyful singing, the crowd eventually emerged from the forest and made their way toward the light they now saw in the distance.

"Come, my brothers. Come closely, my sisters." The crowd could hear Francesco calling them. "See the scene of the nativity of our Lord!" Men reached down to pick up young children as they moved closer to the thin and bent figure that was Francesco. People stared at the unusual sight in front of them, their eyes filled with confusion and delight. Children pointed and mothers hushed noisy exclamations. Had they just been transported to Bethlehem and the actual scene of Christ's birth?

There, in the entrance to a cave, stood a cow and a donkey on either side of a manger filled with hay. The light from several torches cast a romantic glow on the scene and made it almost believable that this was Bethlehem.

Francesco looked into the crowd to see if their faces showed recognition. He smiled when he saw men nodding and the children crowding closer.

"My friends," spoke Francesco, "I want you to behold this scene and think of Christ our Savior. See the great poverty and simplicity of the situation into which he was born. In seeing and experiencing this I want your love for the Christ to deepen beyond anything it was before."

The crowd was quiet as they contemplated what they saw. Soon one of the friars began to recite the mass as Francesco moved to the side to prepare for the sermon. The crowd continued to stand, transfixed by the experience of seeing with their own eyes something they had only been told about in church.

***

Francesco, St. Francis as we now know him, was born in the Italian town of Assisi around 1182 to a wealthy merchant. In medieval times, many people in Italy were Christians. Thus Francesco was baptized as an infant and educated by the church in Assisi.

Francesco grew up as a spoiled son of a rich father. He wore fancy clothing and spent much money on parties with friends. Instead of showing care for the multitude of poor around him in

Assisi, Francesco turned a blind eye to their needs and further indulged himself. He became known as a wild and careless young man, not someone who showed concern for the poor, respect for elders, or honor for Christ.

When Francesco was about twenty years old, Assisi was besieged by a neighboring town, and rich young men like Francesco were taken as prisoners. A year spent in the worst conditions imaginable with little light, no sanitation, no warmth, and insufficient food took its toll on the body and mind of young Francesco. He returned to Assisi to resume his lavish lifestyle, but his body would never again regain its former strength, and his soul was disillusioned with the meaningless life he was leading.

One day Francesco had a vision of what he called "Lady Poverty." When his wild friends inquired if he would soon marry, Francesco replied that he intended to marry Lady Poverty. The poverty of Christ was becoming a theme in Francesco's life. As time went on, he spent fewer days with his partying friends and more and more time in prayer and with poor beggars to whom he would give alms or clothing. He came to

the conclusion that he would never refuse alms to anyone, but rather give willingly and abundantly when asked. Francesco was trading the rich, self-indulgent lifestyle of his youth for a life of poverty and service to others.

Outside of Assisi lay the ruins of a church called San Damiano where Francesco would often go to pray. It was here that he had a vision one day of Christ speaking to him and asking him to repair his house which was falling into ruin.

Francesco assumed this meant he was to rebuild San Damiano and immediately rushed to sell some of his father's merchandise to provide money for the rebuilding of the church. The local priest would not take Francesco's money, and his father was outraged that Francesco would steal from him in this way. The incident caused such an uproar that Francesco hid in a cave for some time before being brought before the town's magistrate for questioning.

At the appointed day, Francesco and his father appeared before the magistrate, surrounded by the people of the town. Francesco returned the bag of money to his father, but then went on to remove

49

his clothing. Handing the garments back to his father, Francesco renounced his family name and place, and he walked out of the town with no clothes and no family connections. Francesco had broken with his former life in every way, resolving only to be connected with the name of Christ and the service of others.

Francesco took up the life of a wandering monk. He vowed to remain poor, to own no property, and have no job but preaching. Francesco preached about following Christ, giving to the poor, pursuing peace, and showing love. He begged for stones, and stone by stone he rebuilt the San Damiano church himself. Others began to join him in his way of life. With permission from the pope in Rome, they became known as the Franciscan order of monks. When a nobleman's daughter from Assisi, Clare,

 50

wanted to join too, Francesco started a group for women which became known as the Poor Clares.

Francesco's life involved much travel: once in order to convert a Sultan to Christianity, and another time to bring an end to the Fifth Crusade. His foremost goal was to preach Christ and show people what Christ was like by his own example. His passion to share Christ was what brought about Francesco's idea of a living nativity scene. Although he had never set foot in Bethlehem, he had in his mind an image of what the first Christmas might have looked like. He loved the songs and stories of troubadours in his youth and had a deep love for animals and nature. Francesco combined these interests with his idea to set up an actual, physical representation of Christ's birth.

Francesco brought the Christmas story to life as an experience that involved hearing, seeing, touching, and even smelling. He had no biblical basis for the inclusion of a cow and a donkey, nor for the backdrop of a cave. We can assume he used these elements because of legends that had developed over the years, or because this was how he imagined the manger scene to look. What Francesco's scene did authentically communicate was the poverty and humility of Christ's birth.

It is hard to know if Francesco was the very first person to re-enact the birth of Christ in this way. Plays depicting biblical stories were popular during the Middle Ages. At first these "mystery plays," as they were called, were performed in church, but by the end of the Middle Ages their content had grown to include material not appropriate for a worship setting. The plays were banned in churches and taken up in village squares instead. Perhaps Francesco used the basic idea behind the original mystery plays to inspire his Christmas drama.

We do know that from the time of St. Francis on, nativity scenes played an important part in the Italian Christmas celebrations and eventually in many other countries as well.

The cloud of darkness that had fallen over Europe during the Middle Ages was beginning to break up. The first glimmers of the dawn of new learning and rediscovery that came with the Renaissance and Reformation were just starting to be appreciated.

Suggested Reading

Philippians 2:3-11; 2 Corinthians 8:9;

Isaiah 53:1-5

Discussion Questions

- How do we see Christ's humility in the circumstances of his birth?

- What do you think of Francis' idea to create a living nativity? Did it help people imagine what it was like when Jesus was born?

- Are there any animals mentioned in the Scriptures as part of the Christmas story?

- How do you learn best? Do you like to listen, look at, or actually do something? Francis wanted his friends to do all three!

- Does your family set up a nativity scene at Christmas time? Why or why not?

- How can you share with those who have less than you?

- Do you find it easy or hard to have a humble attitude?

Enjoy a Soup From Italy

Italy is well known for its delicious food. This soup contains a number of Italian food staples: beans, sausage, kale, and onions. Create a simple dinner of soup and bread and think about Francis' vow of poverty and the compulsion he felt to share with those in need. How can you show love for those in need in your area?

Italian Sausage Soup

Ingredients:

- 4 tbsp./60ml olive oil
- 1 yellow onion, chopped
- 3 large carrots, peeled and chopped
- 2 celery stalks, chopped
- 4 cloves garlic, minced
- 12 oz/400 grams Italian sausage links/spicy pork sausage, cut into slices
- 8 cups/2 liters chicken or vegetable stock
- 1 tsp. dried basil
- 1 tsp. dried oregano

- 1 tsp. dried thyme
- 1 bunch/300-400g kale, chopped and washed
- 15.5oz can/400g tin cannellini beans
- undrained jar of basil pesto to serve

Method:

Heat olive oil in a large pot. Add onion, carrots, and celery. Cook over medium-high heat until onion softens, (8-10 minutes). Stir in the minced garlic and sausage pieces. Allow sausage to brown on the edges. Add the stock to the pan along with the dried herbs. Bring to a boil. Add the chopped kale and cannellini beans. Simmer for about 15 minutes. Season. Serve soup with a spoonful of basil pesto on top of each bowl. Serves 6.

Luther's Protestant Christmas
Wittenberg, Germany, Christmas Eve, 1534

rom heaven high I come to earth, I bring you tidings of great mirth. The first verse of Martin Luther's new hymn rose from lips of the congregation crowded into the Castle Church in Wittenberg. "A little child for you this morn, has from a chosen maid been born," continued the song. A young boy of eight made his way carefully down the aisle with a newborn in his arms. Gently he set the infant into the wooden manger in front of the congregation singing these words as loudly as he could, "Look now, you children, at the sign, a manger cradle far from fine. A tiny baby you will see. Upholder of the world is he."

The boy turned and retreated back down the aisle as the choir of children grouped around the manger burst into song:

> "How glad we'll be if it is so!
> With all the shepherds let us go,
> to see what God for us has done
> in sending us his own dear Son."

The church bells tolled joyfully as the congregation was let out into the cold, crisp air of the German winter. Men and women stood in huddled groups in front of the towering stone church, their children running to and fro with friends.

"Johannes, Magdalena," a strong female voice called out, "Come with me now. We must return home." A young boy and girl scampered up just as a generously built, jolly man in black robes and a hat came marching up to the little group.

"My dear Katherine," called the man with a booming voice, "Let me carry little Martin and Paul, and you carry baby Margarethe." The young boys clinging to their mother's dress were hefted up into the man's arms as the young family made their way out of the square.

"Papa, Papa," cried Magdalena with excitement as the family turned a corner, "Is it almost time for presents?"

"Yes, Papa, please tell us when," added Johannes.

"Don't keep the children in suspense, Martin," chided Katherine, her long, dark skirts blowing in the wind, "Tell them your plan for this evening."

The man named Martin grinned and his eyes twinkled as he looked at each of his children. "Well, now," he began slowly and thoughtfully, "We shall begin by reading the entire book of Romans, and then we will sing ten psalms and five hymns, and then each of you must recite the catechism while I prepare my sermon for tomorrow."

"Papa!" gasped wide-eyed Magdalena, "Is that really what we are to do tonight?"

Martin fixed his grin on the little five-year-old girl beside him. "My dear Lenchen," said Martin as he stooped to place his hand under her chin, "That is only one idea for tonight. What do you say about this idea: when we arrive home we will put some wood into the stove in my study so it grows quite toasty warm in there. We will get your mama to bring in all the wonderful foods she has prepared: the Christmas bread, sausages and roasted meats, chicken pie and bread pudding, mushrooms, sauerkraut, and plenty of beer. We shall sing Christmas hymns and when we've all feasted to our hearts content, I think you will find that the Christkindl may have left some gifts for you."

Magdalene squealed with delight and the little boys clapped their hands. Katherine looked fondly at Martin and broke in, "There will be plenty of students joining us, Martin, and I'm sure we won't end the evening without a little music concert before family worship."

Martin swept his hands in front him as he belted out,

"I can play the whole day long.
I'll dance and sing for you a song,

A soft and soothing lullaby,
so sweet that you will never cry."

Together the family raised their voices to sing in unison the now familiar final verse:

"To God who sent his only Son
Be glory, laud, and honor done.
Let all the choir of heaven rejoice,
the new ring in with heart and voice."

***

It was Christmas Eve in Wittenberg, a small town in Saxony, and Martin Luther was celebrating the day in the festive spirit of both his country upbringing and his commitment to the Christian Church.

Martin was born to humble parents in a small mining town. No one could have guessed he would go on to become one of the most famous men in history, turning the world upside down with his ideas to reform the Church. Martin's father wanted him to study to become a lawyer. Instead, Martin found himself drawn toward the study of theology. Calling out for help in the midst of a treacherous storm in the year 1505, Martin promised to become a monk if he survived. Twelve days later a very alive Martin joined the nearby Augustinian order of monks. Here he took up a life of prayer, biblical study, penance, and pilgrimage. Martin progressed in his theological studies, receiving several degrees, and was put in charge of a number of local monasteries.

In 1511, Martin was sent on monastery business to Rome. It should have been an exciting trip, traveling to the headquarters of the Roman Catholic Church, meeting with the pope, and visiting sites important to church history. Instead, Martin's trip left him heartsick. He found priests who lived openly in sin and made fun of the church services they performed. He saw monks living in luxury rather than caring for the poor. He discovered the highest leaders of the Church failing to practice what the Bible taught. Martin was deeply troubled.

In the late fifteenth century the Church was indeed in need of reforming. Popes with bad theology, poor judgment, and excessive greed had found their way to power in Rome. Indulgences, promising forgiveness of sins, were invented and sold for vast sums to rich and poor alike. The money coffers in Rome grew

judgment to come. Martin prayed, he studied the Bible, and he listened to other mentors and teachers. Finally he came to understand that he could not buy his salvation with money or good works or extreme acts of penance. Salvation was a free gift given by God to those who placed their trust in him.

The state of the Church as a whole continued to bother Martin. On October 31, 1517, Martin took a document he had written and nailed it to the door of the Castle Church in Wittenberg. These 95 Theses, as this document was labeled, called the Church in Rome to change its abusive practices of claiming to sell forgiveness through indulgences and begin reforming the Church away from the many unbiblical practices that had crept in. Uproar, chaos, and danger erupted around Martin because of the 95 Theses. The church

heavy with gold collected from such sales. In 1139, the Church had decreed that priests were no longer allowed to be married. Priests were to be single. However, many priests pretended to be single and secretly kept a mistress. Immorality, greed, and corruption had eaten away at the heart of the church and left a very fragile shell.

Back home in Wittenberg, where Martin lived and taught, he couldn't forget what he had seen in Rome. And he couldn't forget the anguish of his own soul as he wrestled with his sin, God's holiness, and the eternal movement known as the Reformation had begun. Martin was summoned to defend his teachings before representatives of the pope. Later he was excommunicated from the Roman Catholic Church.

The next year Martin was called again to defend himself in the city of Worms before a large gathering of church leaders. Unwilling to recant what he believed Scripture to teach, he was in danger of losing his life. On the way home from Worms, friends kidnapped him and took him to the safety of Wartburg Castle to hide until the furor died down. Here Martin spent his time translating the Bible into German, the language of his people.

As of yet, there were no German Bibles. The Roman Church had decreed mass must be said in Latin, and the Bible was not to be translated into other languages. Martin longed for his people to read the Bible in their own language. Once people could read Scripture, there would be no stopping their demand for change in the Church. Eventually Martin made it safely back to Wittenberg, where he threw himself into teaching and preaching.

As the years passed, and Martin studied Scripture, he began to question the Church's doctrine on priests remaining unmarried. He could not find a biblical basis for this requirement. At the same time, many monks and nuns were leaving the monastic lifestyle, realizing that they could serve God just as well in other vocations. Sometimes Martin helped to find husbands for nuns who left convents and wished to be married.

In 1523, a nun named Katherine von Bora came to Wittenberg. Martin failed to find a husband for Katherine and decided to marry her himself. Martin wanted to show that someone could be both married and a minister of the gospel. In 1525, Martin and Katherine married and took up residence in the old Augustinian monastery. Here, in this long, tall, building with a tower and many windows, the Luthers began their family life.

While Luther lectured and preached, Katherine ran the household, oversaw their farm, and made sure there was food to feed the many guests who came and the needy children they sheltered. Along came six young children of their own. Martin realized they were now living in a very important time for the Church. He realized people all over the world were interested in

what he taught, how he lived, and what he did. Martin wanted what he shared with others to point them to Christ. This was also true of what Martin thought about Christmas.

From all accounts, Martin loved Christmas. Perhaps he had good memories of the country celebrations he enjoyed as a child in his parents' home. During those dark, cold days of December he remembered happy times when people gathered to feast and make music together. No doubt Martin saw Christmas as another way for people to turn their thoughts to Christ. We do know that Martin preached many Christmas sermons. And he wrote several Christmas hymns, including "From Heaven High I Come to You" which was

meant to be part of a Christmas children's pageant. We also know that Martin and Katherine had a happy home life together with their children. Music and singing were a vital part of their family culture, and Martin loved to scoop a child up onto his knee whenever he could.

One way Martin wanted to capture the joy of Christmas for his children was by giving gifts. At this time in Germany, it was popular to give gifts to children on December 6, the feast of St. Nicholas. Martin was concerned that the medieval church's focus on saints

 60

had gone overboard and was edging on saint worship. Because of this, Martin decided to introduce a gift-giving figure to Christmas Eve. He called this figure the "Christkindl" or "Christ child." He hoped that children would better connect Christ with Christmas because of the Christkindl. With Martin's wide influence, the Christkindl became a part of the traditional German Christmas celebration and remains so to this day.

Martin Luther, and all those who ended up leaving the Roman Catholic Church during the Reformation, became known as Protestants because of their protest against the problems in the Medieval Roman Church. Together, the Protestants agreed that change in the church needed to happen, and they agreed that people were granted salvation based on God's gift, not their own good works. However, as we will see, they did not all agree on how Christmas should be celebrated.

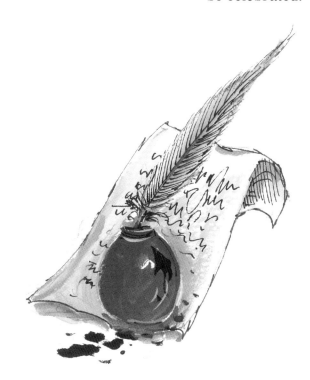

Suggested Reading
Ephesians 2:4-10; Romans 1:16-17

Discussion Questions

- Can you imagine not having a Bible in your own language?

- Do you know any missionaries who are working on Bible translation today?

- Martin Luther particularly loved the book of Romans. What is your favorite book of the Bible?

- Do you open gifts on Christmas Eve or Christmas Day?

- Do you remember who Martin wanted children to associate with the gift-giving?

- Have you ever sung "A Mighty Fortress is Our God?" That is Martin Luther's most famous hymn.

- Does your Christmas resemble the Luthers' Christmas in any way?

Historic German Christmas Cookie

Lebkuchen cookies were developed by German monks in the fourteenth century and are one of the most beloved Christmas treats in Germany today. These cookies are a culinary descendant of Roman honey cookies, and may have been enjoyed by Martin Luther during his Christmas celebrations. Take a bite of these spicy cookies and imagine yourself sitting at the table in the Black Cloister discussing theology with Martin Luther.

Lebkuchen

Ingredients:
- 2 ¼ cup/335g all-purpose flour (plain)
- 1 tsp. ginger
- 1 tsp. cinnamon
- ½ tsp. cloves
- ½ tsp. nutmeg
- ½ tsp. baking soda
- 1 tsp. baking powder
- zest of one lemon
- ⅞ cup/200ml clear honey
- ⅓ cup/85g butter

Glaze:
1 cup/125g confectioner's sugar/icing sugar
2 tbsp. lemon juice
water

Method:

Preheat the oven to 350F/180C/160C Fan. Mix together the flour, spices, baking soda, and baking powder. Add the lemon zest to the flour mixture.

Heat the honey and butter in a pan until the butter is melted. Pour the liquid honey and butter into the flour mixture and stir to combine. Allow to cool slightly.

Form the dough into approximately 30 small balls. Place balls on a greased or parchment paper lined cookie sheet.

Slightly flatten each ball. Bake cookies for 12 minutes until just firm and slightly browned. Cool on wire racks. Mix the glaze ingredients, adding just enough water to form a thin glaze.

When cookies are cool, brush glaze over the tops of the cookies. Allow glaze to dry before putting cookies in an airtight container. Makes about 30 cookies.

Christmas Canceled
England, Christmas Day, 1644

I'm so hungry, complained sixteen-year-old James to his mother as she bustled about the kitchen in her long black dress. "Now James, at your age you shouldn't be complaining. You're a grown man and fully capable of participating in a fast day." James frowned as his younger siblings skipped into the room. "Don't look so glum, James," urged Henry, "dinner is almost ready." James threw an annoyed look at Henry and countered, "You've no right to tell me that when you've taken all your regular meals today."

Young Alice couldn't quite grasp what was going on and called to their mother, "Why hasn't James been eating today, Mother? Is he being punished?" "Of course not my child," called their mother from beside the cooking pot. "James has done nothing bad. Today is a fast day appointed by Parliament. The government asked all those aged sixteen and above to refrain from eating and to spend time in prayer and repentance." James couldn't resist rolling his eyes as he asked, "But why choose Christmas Day for such a fast?" Mother sighed as she turned from the pot back to the work table. "My children, you know the Bible does not command the celebration of Christ's birth, and you know that this time of year is typically filled with drunken brawls in the streets and careless and harmful behavior. Parliament wishes to put an end to the waste and mischief and needless destruction that takes place on this day."

The children ate in silence at the evening meal, careful to exercise their manners and listen attentively to the adults as they talked. "Was the fast day successful, Brother Peter?" asked father in his booming voice after the blessing was said and a portion of Psalm 145 sung. "I didn't see many drunks roaming about," began Peter, "but there was nearly a riot among the shops. Some folks were upset that the shops were open for business on Christmas Day, and before we knew it, men were fighting in the streets."

Father shook his head and took a hungry bite of the mutton stew. "Christmas seems to cause nothing but trouble here in England. Perhaps our friends in the Massachusetts Bay colony have it better." The children watched as Uncle Peter scooped more bean pottage onto his plate and took a long swig of ale. "There is something to be said for that, Robert. No Christmas services in their churches, no legal day off work, and no memories of such things to tempt their children. Perhaps the New World will be better off without the disorder and disturbances of Christmas that we've experienced."

James kept his gaze on his food but his thoughts floated away from the dimly lit room to the scene he'd witnessed that afternoon. He'd happened to glance up out of the side yard toward their neighbor's house in time to see an older man slip silently in their back door. At another time that afternoon, with his senses heightened from the lack of food, James was sure he'd caught a whiff of the sweet and spicy scent of mince pies floating in the breeze. He'd brushed the idea off as his imagination gone wild, knowing mince pies would quickly alert the authorities to a prohibited Christmas feast. Now he wasn't so sure. Maybe he had smelled mince pies. Maybe his neighbors were actually Catholics and that man he'd seen was a priest coming in secret to perform a forbidden Christmas mass.

***

It was 1644 in England. Christmas was outlawed by Parliament and replaced with a solemn fast day. Gone were the golden days of the Tudor Christmases when the king's court observed the twelve days of Christmas with every ounce of gaiety and revelry possible. The trappings of a late medieval English Christmas had retreated into the shadows: no boar's head, no wassail, no Christmas pies, no mistletoe, no Lords of Misrule, no singing of carols or plays in the streets. Parliament was hoping Christmas would disappear.

The Reformation years, which followed the Middle Ages, were years during which many Christians began examining the Church's practices against Scripture to see if what the Church was doing was truly biblical. Some reformers, like Martin Luther, felt that celebrating Christmas was a marvelous way to honor Christ and enjoy happy times with family and friends. Other men, like John Knox in Scotland, could find no command in Scripture to celebrate Christ's birth. Knox argued that the absence of a recorded birth date in the Bible was further evidence that we should not celebrate this holiday taken from pagan origins. John Calvin, the reformer living in Geneva, Switzerland, felt it was not something to fight about. If individual churches wanted to celebrate the nativity of Christ in their worship service, they should feel free to do so. If some churches felt it was not right, they should refrain

from celebrating. Romans 14:5-6 provided guidelines for this argument: "One person esteems one day as better than another, while another esteems all days alike. Each one should be fully convinced in his own mind. The one who observes the day, observes it in honor of the Lord. The one who eats, eats in honor of the Lord, since he gives thanks to God, while the one who abstains, abstains in honor of the Lord and gives thanks to God."

Religious reformation took England by a storm in the early 1500s. The teachings of men such as Martin Luther, Ulrich Zwingli, and John Calvin jumped the Channel and slowly made their way into English minds. Men and women began to question many of the practices of the Medieval Church, practices like buying forgiveness, preventing commoners from having a Bible in their own language, tolerating immoral behavior of priests, and enriching the monasteries to the detriment of the poor. People were upset. They wanted the Bible in English. They wanted a reformation of the churches in England.

The trouble brewing in the English churches came to a head when King

Henry VIII argued with the pope over a divorce from his first wife. Henry wanted a male heir and his wife had only produced a female child. Henry was convinced he had done something sinful by marrying his brother's widow. He demanded a divorce so he could escape his "sinful marriage" and marry someone else. The pope would not agree to Henry's divorce. Henry decided on a bold act. In 1534, he renounced the Church of Rome and the leadership of the pope and declared himself the Head of the English Church! The churches in England would no longer be Catholic but Anglican.

It would take many years for the new Anglican Church to work out exactly what it felt the Bible taught. And there would be a period of reverting to Catholicism under the rule of Henry's daughter, Mary. Eventually, with Queen Elizabeth I, Protestant churches (churches that are not Catholic) would take a firm hold in England. Catholicism would be outlawed as a treasonous act of allegiance to a leader other than England's king or queen. It was a tumultuous time when many feared for their lives because of their religious beliefs.

Things worsened when Charles Stuart took the throne in 1625. Charles believed that he was divinely appointed by God to be King of England and should therefore have no accountability to Parliament or the people. He was a tyrannical ruler, taxing the country without the approval of Parliament and making rash decisions. Charles' leadership as Head of the English Church also caused problems. He leaned more toward Catholicism and tried to push his religious viewpoint on both England and Scotland with disastrous results.

Eventually, Parliament had enough. They took matters into their own hands to curb the power of King Charles. Parliament decided not only to lessen the king's power, but to pass legislation intended to make England a better country. Some of these parliamentary acts dealt with the Church of England, its beliefs, and its celebrations. Christmas was banned in an effort to end the drunkenness, mischief, and social disruption it caused.

Many people were happy to do away with Christmas and its dark side. But many commoners were upset. They loved their Christmas revelries and traditions. They didn't mind giving up the Christmas church services, but they wanted to keep their Christmas foods and traditions. Many people wanted Christmas back. But it wasn't until 1660, when Charles II took up the throne, that the Christmas ban was lifted.

In the midst of all this political turmoil in England, there was a group that continued to celebrate Christmas religiously: the Catholics. Although they were banned from worshiping publicly, many Catholics conducted secret worship in their houses. Itinerant priests traveled covertly from house to house, holding mass for its inhabitants. Many wealthy Catholics built secret hiding places for priests in their homes. It was a very difficult time for Catholics because they risked imprisonment or execution if they were discovered.

Meanwhile, a large number of English Christians, known as Puritans because of their desire to purify the Church, had emigrated to the New World in search of religious freedom. They left their Christmas celebrations behind in England and observed and enforced December 25 as an ordinary work day in their new colony. The Puritans hoped to do away with the pagan origins of Christmas as well as keep their children from the drunkenness and disruption that occurred on this day. Eventually, as the centuries passed, Christmas celebrations would trickle into America, but the Puritan influence lingered well into the eighteenth century.

Suggested Reading

Colossians 2:16-17; I Corinthians 10:31

Discussion Questions

- Why did Parliament cancel Christmas?
- What are some of the ways Christmas can cause problems today?
- Do you know someone who doesn't celebrate Christmas?
- How could you show respect for someone who chooses not to celebrate Christmas?
- How would you react if you had to fast on Christmas Day?
- What is one thing that might be good to change about the way Christmas is celebrated today?
- What would you miss most if Christmas was canceled?

Mince Pie Flavors

Mince Pies began their development in the thirteenth century when crusaders brought spices back from the Middle East. The pies started as a savory dish that included dried fruits and spices. Today the savory meat is gone; all we have left is a pastry shell with a filling of spiced, dried fruits. As the pie developed, it became one of the most recognizable symbols of a British Christmas. These cookies capture the taste of mince pies without all the work of preparing pastry and filling. Discuss how Christmas can help strengthen your spiritual life, rather than discourage it, as you taste the flavors of a British Christmas.

Mince Pie Cookies

Ingredients:
- ½ cup/70g dried cranberries
- ½ cup/70g raisins
- ½ cup/70g golden raisins/sultanas
- ½ cup/70g dried currants
- 2 tbsp. brandy (optional)
- 2 ¼ cup/335g all-purpose flour (plain)
- 1 tsp. baking soda
- 1 tsp. salt
- 1 tsp. cinnamon
- ½ tsp. nutmeg
- ½ tsp. cloves
- ½ tsp. allspice
- 1 cup/113g butter, softened
- ¾ cup/150g brown sugar
- ¾ cup/150g white sugar
- zest of one lemon and one orange
- 1 tsp. vanilla
- 2 eggs

Method:

Preheat oven to 350F/180C/160C Fan. Place dried fruits in a small bowl and sprinkle with brandy if using. Set aside. In a medium bowl, combine flour, baking soda, salt, and spices. Set aside. In the bowl of a stand mixer, cream together the butter and sugars. Add the vanilla, orange zest, and lemon zest. Beat in the eggs one at a time, scraping down the sides of the bowl in between. Mix in the flour mixture and then the dried fruit mixture.

Drop cookie dough by rounded spoons onto greased or parchment paper lined cookie sheets. Bake for 10-12 minutes until lightly browned and almost firm. Cool on racks. Makes about 48.

Christmas and America
Williamsburg, Virginia, Christmas Day, 1774

Eleanor woke with a start. The rapid musket fire in her ears was rattling the windows and causing her heart to pound. Seconds later, it registered: today was Christmas Day! A smile spread across her face and she leaned her head back against the pillow with a sigh of relief. The shots she heard were just the local men welcoming this special day and the beginning of the twelve days of Christmas.

Donning her many petticoats, Eleanor then pulled her best dress over her head. Aunt Martha had promised Christmas Day here in Williamsburg would be special. Dashing out the door, Eleanor paused before setting foot on the staircase. She remembered she must act like the lady of fifteen that she was. Slowly she descended the stairs, admiring the carved flowers adorning the intricate woodwork and pretending she was the English governor's daughter about to receive visitors below.

A boy with tousled brown hair flew by the staircase. "Josiah," hissed Eleanor. "Slow down! This isn't the country, boy. Mind your manners!" Josiah slowed enough for Eleanor to catch up with him. As they approached the dining room, William, one of the enslaved members of the household, opened the door with a grin. Inside sat Aunt Martha at the polished oval table with Uncle Isaac and Great Uncle Thomas. "Come and sit down my dears," she called, motioning them to the two chairs on either side of her.

Eleanor and Josiah took their seats at the table and bowed their heads as Great Uncle Thomas offered the morning prayer. When the children opened their eyes they spied candy at the top of their places. Eleanor stifled a squeal of delight, but Josiah made his pleasure known loud and clear.

"Well, it is Christmas after all," said Great Uncle Thomas. "Your Aunt Martha thought you would enjoy a little treat." Eleanor's eyes shone. She'd never received anything special on Christmas before.

Uncle Isaac, who had not yet spoken, suddenly volunteered, "I imagine Christmas will be celebrated in as many different ways today as there are houses in Williamsburg. It will be quite the party at the Governor's Mansion, and your aunt has her own dinner and festivities planned." He paused to clear his throat, then continued, "I'm sure there won't be a peep out of the Presbyterians today. They'll be busy going about their usual business." Aunt Martha, who didn't want to imagine life without Christmas festivities, waved her hand at the window and said, "Well, leave them to their work. We are going to have ourselves a very happy time indeed."

As the children spooned the hot breakfast porridge and maple sugar to their mouths Aunt Martha broke in, "Now my darlings, we need to be ready to go to church by half past ten. Bruton Parish is bound to be full today for the Christmas service and I want to make sure we arrive in plenty of time."

Aunt Martha stopped talking just long enough to take a sip of her coffee. "My, how I miss tea," she continued with a shake of her head. "Why do the British have to be so obstinate about taxes. Just imagine the breakfast next door at the Governor's Palace this morning: as much hot tea as anyone could drink accompanied by toast and biscuits and fresh bread, and...."

"Now, now," broke in Great Uncle Thomas, "Let's not have any unpatriotic talk in my house. It's important we act in solidarity with those in Boston, especially considering my history as mayor of this town." Aunt Martha twitched in her chair like a hen fluffing her feathers, but meekly picked up her coffee and said not a word more of tea.

It was still cold and frosty when the family gathered to walk the short distance to Bruton Parish Church. The smells of roasting hams and turkeys, baking breads and pies, wafted slowly around them, helping to mask the normal stench of horse and pig dung that had a way of clinging to the streets of Williamsburg. Eleanor noticed the pretty hemlock and fir swags decorating doors and windows of some of the houses they passed, and Josiah's eyes darted to the large quantity of schoolboys walking the streets.

Aunt Martha seemed to sense Josiah's observations and volunteered, "The school-boys are tired of their studies and have locked the schoolmasters out of the College of William and Mary. I expect they hope for a few days' vacation."

While the rector led the congregation in the Christmas service, Eleanor couldn't help her mind wandering to the festivities ahead. Later today would be the Christmas dinner and they could indulge in all the delicious foods Eleanor had glimpsed in the kitchen: ham, turkey, venison, stuffing, biscuits, cornbread, pickles, squash, vegetables of several kinds, fruit pies, mince pies, and plum pudding! She could hardly wait!

Aunt Martha had kept their meals simple leading up to this day in an effort to observe the fast of Advent as the Anglican church decreed. She could be so very English at times, thought Eleanor. There was to be a Yule log set on fire in the drawing room and there was talk of going to a dance at a nearby house in the evening. Eleanor tried to count the parties Aunt Martha had mentioned would be taking place in the next twelve days. She knew they'd be going to Great Uncle Thomas' house in the country at some point during the week for the fox-hunting and there was a wedding to attend on January 6. Eleanor could hardly contain her excitement for the days ahead, and thought what good fortune it was that her parents had allowed Josiah and herself to come visit Williamsburg. A sharp pinch followed by a stern look brought her back to the present. Eleanor jumped to her feet as the congregation stood for the closing prayer and benediction, silently murmuring her own thanks to God for this special season.

***

Christmas in the colony of Virginia was an entirely different picture from what took place in the northern colonies. Following the example of the Puritans in seventeenth century England, Christmas had been illegal for many years in places like the Massachusetts Bay colony. As the colonies grew and the population expanded to include immigrants from other

75

religious groups and countries, so the views of Christmas changed and expanded. It truly was a time in which Christmas might be celebrated (or not) in 100 different ways throughout the New World.

Williamsburg, Virginia was the center of Virginian culture and government from 1699 to 1780. Being a colony of Great Britain, Williamsburg was heavily influenced by British culture. The city had a British governor and an Anglican church. Its citizens walked the streets in the latest British fashions complete with powdered wigs and masses of gold brocade. The Anglican Bruton Parish church set a very different religious tone than that of the more conservative Puritan-influenced churches in the north. There was also a great deal of nostalgia for the celebrations and practices of Old England here in the South. All this combined to make Christmas celebrations common and festive in Williamsburg.

For many people in Williamsburg, Christmas was a season, not just a special day. Christmas Day marked the beginning of twelve days of revelry and feasting. It was an adult-focused holiday season celebrating the end of the hard work of harvest. There were many wealthy landowners in Virginia and these families hosted fox hunts, festive balls, and elaborate feasts. It was also a popular time for weddings, since people were already gathered together. Houses were decorated with greens such as holly, ivy, and laurel. Mince pies, plum puddings, and gingerbread graced the tables. Turkeys, hams, venison, and roast beef filled the larders. The abundant harvest created by Virginia's rich soil made the Christmas season one of plenty.

All this merriment was made possible because of the many enslaved persons such wealthy families owned. Slavery was still legal in both Great Britain and the colonies, and it was the work of these men, women, and children that made possible the rich harvests of tobacco and cotton in Virginia. In fact, Williamsburg at this time, was home to more enslaved persons than free. Few considered the inequality of enjoying luxury at the expense of another's freedom, and it would be nearly 100 more years before slavery was abolished in America.

Christmas for those in slavery was very different than for those living in freedom. There was extra work to put on all the parties and prepare the enormous quantities of food required. If the enslaved person belonged to an accommodating family, he or she might be given some time off at Christmas to visit relatives. This could be the only chance in the year to see a husband or wife, child or parent. Because of this, Christmas became a longed-for day for many living in slavery. In addition to time off, they might even receive a coin or two from the master, or maybe a jug of ale.

Many enslaved persons were deeply religious. If Christmas Day could not be a day of fun and relaxation, it could be a day to remember their Savior and gather at night in cabins to sing of their joys and sorrows.

Not everyone was wealthy or enslaved. There were many families who fell in the middle class. They, too, celebrated Christmas at whatever level their income allowed. School-boys might bar their teacher from entering the schoolhouse and thus create a school holiday for themselves. Yule logs were available to anyone with access to a forest. Wild turkeys could be hunted, along with deer, providing extra meat for a special meal. The point was to find a way to bring happiness and joy to what otherwise might be the darkest and most depressing time of the year.

Christmas in the eighteenth century was still not focused on children. It was centered around adults and their balls, feasts, and fox hunts. Presents for children were rare, except perhaps in German households where the Christkindl made his appearance. A few youngsters might find some candy set aside for them, or a small coin, but no filled stockings or pile of presents. Children were bystanders to this adult-centered holiday and would remain so well into the nineteenth century when the Victorians changed Christmas forever.

Suggested Reading

Romans 12:9-18; John 13:34-35

Discussion Questions

- How is a Williamsburg Christmas similar to your Christmas? How is it different?

- What do you think about Christmas being adult-focused in the 1700s?

- God's Word urges us to give thanks in all circumstances. What can you be thankful for at Christmas?

- Have you ever been to a Christmas party? Do you think it had any similarities to a Williamsburg Christmas party?

- Do you go to church on, or near, Christmas?

- Could you sit at a meal and not speak unless spoken to?

- If you were a slave, would you be excited for Christmas? Why or why not?

24 Ways to Celebrate a Williamsburg Christmas

1. Decorate your house with fresh evergreens and holly
2. Attend church and observe the fast of Advent
3. Drink hot chocolate spiced with cinnamon and nutmeg
4. Plan a large feast with many different dishes
5. Make an edible centerpiece for your table from citrus fruit
6. Get together with friends to sing Christmas carols
7. Consider exchanging gifts on New Year's Day
8. Scent your house with dried lavender, rose petals, and rosemary
9. Host an informal concert
10. Play games together as a family
11. Stretch your Christmas celebrations to cover two months
12. Host a party on Twelfth Night
13. Attend a wedding
14. Bake a Twelfth Night Cake
15. Enjoy Christmas wassail (non-alcoholic)
16. Spend an evening sitting in front of a real fire
17. Take a ride in a horse and carriage
18. Eat dinner by candlelight
19. Prepare roast beef or bake a ham for Christmas dinner
20. Enjoy a break from school
21. Bake gingerbread cookies
22. Give up drinking tea
23. Invite houseguests to stay with you for Christmas
24. Bake and eat plum pudding and mince pies

79

Christmas Reinvented
London, Christmas, 1850

*A*nd it was always said of him, that he knew how to keep Christmas well, if any man alive possessed the knowledge. May that be truly said of us, and all of us! And so, as Tiny Tim observed, God Bless Us, Every one!

Squeals erupted from the eight children crowded around the open book. "God bless us, every one!" cried six-year-old Frank with feeling as his father tousled his hair.

"Am I the age of Tiny Tim, Father?" questioned five-year-old Alfred.

"Perhaps you are, son," replied his father. "Come now children, let's go into the parlor and have a look at our Christmas tree." The sound of so many excited young feet clattering on the floor put a smile on the face of their father as he lifted the baby to his arms and followed.

A fire blazed in the immense marble fireplace of the parlor. Next to the fire stood an evergreen tree propped against the wall and covered in white candles and candy.

"Mr. Dickens, sir," came a timid voice. "Is it time to light the candles, sir?"

The man holding the baby turned to face the speaker. "If we can just keep the children away long enough, I think we can light the candles," replied Mr. Dickens to the housemaid.

At that moment Mrs. Dickens raised her voice, "Children, please sit down," she called over the mayhem, motioning with her arms for them to sit. "Sit down so we can light the candles and pass out the gifts."

Carefully, Mr. Dickens began to light the candles on the tree. As the glow brightened the dark room, the children fell into an awed hush. Foil-wrapped candy glinted in the soft light, and the older children counted enough pieces hanging from the tree for each child to receive a sizable handful.

Out of the stillness came Mrs. Dickens' comforting voice as she began to sing: "The holly and the ivy, when they are both full grown."

Slowly the children joined in as they sat mesmerized by the spectacular sight before them. There was one perfect moment of silence when the song finished before the children burst out again, "Now Father, give us the presents now, please!"

Mr. Dickens smiled as he reached below the tree to grasp the first paper-wrapped present. Grandfather and Grandmother Dickens sat on the sofa by the fire, observing the proceedings with amused approval.

"Children," called Mr. Dickens some time later, "there will be more time tomorrow to play with your new toys. It's nearly time to go in for our Christmas dinner."

Shouts and exclamations began all over again. "We'll have turkey, Father," shouted Walter. "And Christmas pie," added Kate. "I want an orange," said twelve-year-old Mary in a wistful tone. "And we can pull the crackers," yelled Frank as he jumped up and down in front of his mother.

"Do calm down a bit, Frank," admonished Mrs. Dickens. "I want you to be on your best behavior when we sit at the table." Mrs. Dickens glanced at her husband. "What, Charles," asked Mrs. Dickens with a twinkle in her eye, "will be your favorite part of the meal?"

"Why, my dear, you know the answer to that. It will be the enormous Christmas pudding that's been boiling away in the copper all this afternoon."

***

It was 1850 in Victorian London and the Dickenses were about to sit down to their traditional Christmas dinner. Christmas was no longer a remnant from the past observed by street ruffians hoping for a bit of fun, or wealthy lords in their manors devouring boar's head at long tables. Christmas was different now. It had been reinvented. The Christmas of 1850 reflected the Victorian values of beautiful surroundings, abundant provisions, and endearing home life. It meant heaps of decorations, a new-fangled Christmas tree complete with candles and candy, a large dinner centered on a goose or turkey, piles of gifts purchased from stores or made by hand, Christmas cards and Christmas crackers, and the ever-popular Christmas pudding.

It was a world away from the simple and austere celebrations, or lack of celebration, in the 1700s. It was the simple power of the written word that had made the change.

First came Washington Irving, an American author fascinated with England and intent on writing about old-fashioned, English Christmases. His books were popular, and the scenes he painted so vivid, that people took them for reality, not the fiction they were. Everyone wanted a Christmas like Irving described, and they saw no reason not to have one. Soon Christmas in the British Isles looked like Christmas in Irving's books, and everyone thought they were faithfully recreating real history.

Charles Dickens jumped into the action when he published his extremely popular book, *A Christmas Carol*. Victorians were in love with Tiny Tim, the ailing son of Bob Cratchit, an overworked London clerk. Readers despised the likes of Ebenezer Scrooge who made Mr. Cratchit work on Christmas (forgetting the fact that most people in Victorian times still worked on Christmas). Those touched by the book vowed to show charity to the poor and generosity to others during the Christmas season. Christmas was leaving the religious focus of worship and adoration of Christ, and finding a secular focus in charity, generosity, and time spent with one's children.

Children were, for the first time in history, the center of the Christmas celebration. The tree was for their enjoyment, the presents were for their pleasure, the games and activities prepared to keep them happily entertained. Adults still enjoyed their Christmas drinks and the Christmas dinner, and might even exchange a small present or two, but most of the time and expense was devoted to giving children a magical experience.

The Victorians had more money and leisure time than people in past centuries.

Christmas festivities were a chance for using this extra time and money. Hours could be spent meticulously covering green peas in red wax to create holly berries for decorations, or folding and pasting paper into intricate ornaments. There was time to fashion colored paper into fancy Christmas chains, or stitch embroidered handkerchiefs as presents. The Industrial Revolution made mass-produced toys

something people could afford as gifts. Shops became a wonderland of Christmas goods and gimmicks.

With the immigration of many Germans to Great Britain and America, the Christmas tree burst into popularity. When Prince Albert and Queen Victoria were shown standing around their Christmas tree with their young children, a surge in the annual sales of Christmas trees took place. Christmas cards began to be printed and sold, and within decades were an established tradition. Tom Smith of London invented the first Christmas crackers in 1847. These were paper-wrapped tubes containing trinkets and candies and were pulled open at the Christmas dinner table by each guest.

Christmas dinner had changed a bit since medieval times. Boar's head was no longer of interest to the vast middle class to whom Christmas now belonged. Goose was the meat of choice, followed quickly by turkey which Charles Dickens made famous in his *A*

Christmas Carol. Christmas pie was a popular dish consisting of pastry filled with chicken or turkey, and game birds such as partridge, pigeon, or pheasant. Mince pies began to leave the meat out and gradually became more dried fruit focused. Wassailing had all but died away, and in its place had come a glass of Christmas sherry or perhaps some rum punch. Christmas pudding continued to be enjoyed by all as a classic part of an English Christmas.

Christmas music took a great leap forward during Victorian times. Christmas carols grew in popularity, and many new carols were written. Hymn books in Britain and America began to include more Christmas carols, making them easily accessible to the public. Piano playing and group singing were popular and often became a part of a family's evening entertainment after Christmas dinner.

Christmas still had a religious element to it with sacred Christmas music being sung and church services conducted. However, the religious emphasis of Christ's birth began to take a back seat to cultural traditions. Concern for the poor was encouraged, and Christmas as a season of good works and goodwill was promoted with positive results. People acknowledged Christ's birth at Christmas, but it was not the center of celebration.

What happened in London soon happened across the ocean in America. Magazines, newspapers, and personal letters carried the British Christmas traditions to Canada and the recently formed United States of America. Soon Christmas trees, Christmas cards, and store-bought presents filled the homes of Americans from north to south as they opened their arms wide to embrace in a new way this Christmas holiday.

The invention of the Victorian Christmas laid the groundwork for Christmas as we now know it in the twenty-first century. From Christmas shopping, to Christmas dinner, to watching *A Christmas Carol* on television, men, women, and children now carry on the traditions the Victorians developed from reading fictionalized Christmas stories. As the Victorian period came to a close, there was a major Christmas personality destined to dominate the twentieth century who was just beginning to come into his own: Santa Claus.

Suggested Reading

I Timothy 6:17-19; Hebrews 10:24

Discussion Questions

- God encourages those who have much to share with those who have little. How can you share with others at Christmas?

- What should motivate our generosity to others?

- Why do you think it is easy to forget about Jesus when life is good and we have many blessings?

- Are there people you know of who could use your help at Christmas?

- Do you see similarities between your Christmas and the Victorian Christmas?

- Have you read or watched *A Christmas Carol*? What did you think of it?

- What is your favorite Christmas carol?

Make Victorian Christmas Decorations

Orange Pomander

Create a clove-studded orange and enjoy its aromatic scent just as Victorian families used pleasant scents to distract them from the not-so-nice smells of everyday living.

You will need: One whole orange, whole cloves

Instructions: Poke holes in an orange about 1 cm apart from each other in a pretty design. Place a whole clove in each hole. After covering your orange with cloves, tie a ribbon around it and hang in a prominent place.

Paper Chain

The Victorians enjoyed making Christmas decorations out of paper and glue. The paper chain is a simple decoration that points back to the time when Christmas decor was made almost entirely by hand.

You will need: Strips of colored paper approximately 1 inch/2.5cm by 8 inches/20cm, staples or tape

Instructions: Use staples or pieces of tape to form a circle from the first piece of paper. Link the next strip of paper through the first loop and close it into a circle. Continue linking circles until a long chain is created.

Gingerbread Cookie Tree Decorations

Use a favorite gingerbread cookie recipe to bake gingerbread cookies to hang on your tree. When you cut the cookies out, be sure to poke a large hole that won't close with baking into each cookie. Bake your cookies slightly longer than usual. When cool, thread ribbon or yarn through the holes in your cookies and hang them on your tree.

From St. Nicholas to Santa Claus

Oklahoma Territory, December 24, 1896

Now John, I want you to sit right here at this table and begin threading popcorn with the needle and thread. Charles, come and help with the popcorn garland too. We need as many yards as we can to decorate the tree.

"What kind of tree are we having this year, Mama?" inquired John as he took his seat and picked up the threaded needle.

"Your father tells me he has cut a large Sage Brush tree and will have it set up in the front of the mission hall later this afternoon," replied Mrs. Osborne. "It's not quite an evergreen, but it's the best we can do out here in the Territory."

Mrs. Osborne bustled over to the other end of the table where two girls were carefully pasting colorful paper chains together. "Good work, girls. I'm going to open up the barrels that came from out East and make sure we have enough presents for everyone in attendance tonight.

Mrs. Osborne carefully pried the lid off two enormous shipping barrels that were sitting to one side of the room. "It's a mercy these arrived in time," she said with a sigh. "I don't know what we would have done if the train had been delayed another day. Why, here's a letter from your Aunt Ethel, children."

"Oh, tell us what she says, Mama," urged the girls.

Mrs. Osborne smiled and obligingly opened the letter to read, "Dear Sister," began Mrs. Osborne, "I hope this letter finds each of you well and anticipating Christmas and the arrival of Santa Claus. Here in the East everyone is in a flurry wherever I go. Dashing here, shopping there, moaning about the rising cost of keeping Christmas. Can you imagine, few people want to make their Christmas gifts these days! Everyone wants to buy, buy, buy. I miss our childhood when everything we received was carefully sewn by mother at night, or carved by father in the woodshed."

"She should move out West," broke in Charles. "We still have to make most of our presents out here!" Mrs. Osborne nodded and continued, "Our congregation managed to collect enough candy for everyone at your mission to have one bag each. And I counted twice to make sure the knitted socks, hats, and scarves were the quantities you mentioned for placing on the community tree. Florence insisted we send your family two fruitcakes and some of our very own maple candy. I also found a few Christmas Annuals from last year which I thought

you and the children would enjoy reading through. A very happy Christmas to you all. Love, Aunt Ethel." Mrs. Osborne looked wistful as she set the letter down.

"Do you miss Christmas in the East, Mama?" asked Helen as she picked up the next piece of colored paper. Mrs. Osborne thought for a moment. "I miss the people, Helen, but our Christmas here is just as special: our roast chicken dinner is just like back East, and we'll have Aunt Ethel's fruitcake to enjoy, and the mincemeat pies I made yesterday. Father will stay home from the store, and tonight we'll all go to the mission to sing Christmas carols, watch the Christmas play you children are putting on, and share these gifts from the barrels with everyone who comes. And we mustn't forget about Santa Claus!"

At the mention of Santa Claus the boys jumped up and down in their seats and tried without success to suppress their squeals. "We need cookies to leave for Santa Claus, Mama," begged Charles. "But what about the snow," asked John with a sudden worried look on this face. "How can Santa Claus come without snow?" Mrs. Osborne patted John's head as she replied, "You mustn't worry about Santa Claus. Out here in the Territory, he will borrow a horse and wagon if he needs to. What you need to worry about is being good. Remember Santa Claus only leaves presents in the stockings of good little boys and girls." "Yes, Mama," cried the children in chorus, and bent their heads quickly to their tasks.

***

It was 1896 in the American West. Here Christmas was less elaborate, without the excesses that had taken over celebrations in Eastern America and Britain. Men and women worked to make the day special: a bigger meal than usual, a simple, homemade gift, or a gathering shared with neighbors. For children, it was Santa Claus who captured their attention. Had they been good enough to merit a present in their stocking, or would their mischievous deeds catch up with them?

Santa Claus, this larger-than-life character who had suddenly become a fixture of Christmas, began his evolution nearly 1600 years before in the life of Nicholas, Bishop of Myra, in what is now modern-day Turkey.

Few historical facts are known about Nicholas. Nothing was written about him until nearly four hundred years after his death. What we do know is that around the time of A.D. 270-343, there was a Nicholas who was a bishop (a priest or pastor) in the Myra area, he may have been at the Council of Nicea in A.D. 325, and his life became the subject of legends over the next 900 years. To confuse matters further, two hundred years after Nicholas of Myra died there was another Nicholas: Nicholas of Sion. The life details of these two Nicholas'

91

became entwined and it is difficult to know now which details belong to which life.

During the medieval years it was a common practice to compile a written "Life" of various Christian men and women. This "Life" would tell details about the person: both true and embellished. This was not intended to mislead people but rather encourage believers in their faith. The authors hoped their readers would admire these holy men and women of old and seek to act the same way.

As Nicholas' life story developed over the years, a certain legend became connected with him: the story of a poor man with three daughters. Many versions have been told, but the heart of the story involves a man who can no longer care for his daughters and fears he must sell them into slavery. Nicholas hears of the man's troubles and decides a good use of the money he inherited from his Christian parents would be to help him. Quietly, at night, Nicholas goes to the man's house and throws a sack of gold coins in the window. The gold coins land in an empty shoe (or stocking, or down the chimney). The man is utterly amazed and can't believe he now has money to marry off his first daughter respectably. Nicholas repeats his actions two more times in order to provide for all three daughters.

With this legend, Nicholas, now called St. Nicholas, began to be known for kindness and generosity to children. December 6, the legendary death date of Nicholas, became the yearly remembrance of this godly man's life. As time went on, gifts began to be given to children on December 6 in his memory. By the end of the Middle Ages, St. Nicholas had a huge following all over Europe and beyond. December 6 was a well-established Roman Catholic and Eastern Orthodox feast day. St. Nicholas was pictured as a man in long robes with a staff and a mitre on his head: the traditional dress of a Christian bishop.

The reformation of the Church in the 1500s caused a hiccup in the celebration of St. Nicholas' Day. Protestants, like Martin Luther in Germany, were concerned that too much emphasis was given to the saints, taking attention away from Christ. Luther proposed that St. Nicholas' Day be given up, and the tradition of giving presents to children be transferred to the Christ Child bringing presents on Christmas Eve. In England, the celebration of many saint's days trickled out as the Church separated from the Roman Catholic Church and became the Church of England. A Christmas gift-bringer, in the form of a man in a long robe called Father Christmas, entered the English Christmas. In the Netherlands, there was a rich history of Saint Nicholas, or Sinter Klaas as he was known. Sinter Klaas apparently spent the year in Spain and arrived in the Netherlands by boat each year to bring presents to children on December 6. The Reformation years brought a pause in these celebrations when people stopped observing saints' days. Sinter Klaas returned to popularity in the 1800s but without as much religious connection.

St. Nicholas next appeared in the early 1800s in America. In 1809, a few men in New York City got together to form the New York Historical Society. New York had originally been settled by people from the Netherlands and the founders of the Historical Society decided, for some reason, that St. Nicholas would be a good symbol of New York's Dutch roots. That same year, Washington Irving, the great American writer, published a comical history of New York in which he stressed the importance of St. Nicholas to the early settlers of the city. Irving's history was a joke, not based on fact, but his word pictures of St. Nicholas sliding down chimneys and flying over trees stuck in people's heads.

Fourteen years after Irving's *History* was published, an anonymous poem was printed entitled, "A Visit from St. Nicholas" (now known as "A Night Before Christmas.") The poem described St. Nicholas in great detail. He had a sleigh and reindeer and his gift-giving took place not on December 6 but on Christmas Eve. The robes of a Christian bishop were gone, and in their place were ash and soot-tarnished furs. Soon the Dutch name for St. Nicholas — Sinter Klaas — took on an American pronunciation: Santa Claus!

By the mid-1800s, people had learned more of what Santa Claus looked like from the drawings of a magazine cartoonist named Thomas Nast. Each year Nast would draw pictures of Santa Claus to be published, and each year new details would emerge: a jolly face, beard, and wide belt; a

fur hat and the base location of the North Pole; a toyshop and elf helpers; letters and a ledger for keeping track of good and bad children; and of course the necessity of leaving a snack for Santa's arrival.

By the end of the 1800s, Santa Claus had taken the English-speaking world by storm! Everyone talked about Santa and children worked hard to be good lest they receive coal instead of presents on Christmas morning. The importance of Santa Claus judging a child's behavior was ever present, and provided a useful tool for tired parents who wanted their children to behave during the holiday season.

Although everyone was now agreed on who Santa Claus was, what he did, and where he came from (the North Pole), there was still disparity on what he looked like. Sometimes he had robes, or a fur coat. The coat could be yellow, or red and white. Finally, in the 1930s, Haddon Sundblom painted Santa Claus in a red and white suit for the Coca-Cola advertisements. This consolidated the modern image of Santa. Santa was now fully defined as the great gift-giver of Christmas. Once again, Christmas was moving away from a religious celebration to a fully commercialized and secular celebration.

Suggested Reading

James 1:17; Matthew 7:11

Discussion Questions

- Who is the ultimate giver of every good gift?
- What did St. Nicholas come to be known for?
- The Legend of St. Nicholas tells of Nicholas' desire to help others in great need. How can you help those in need at Christmas time?
- Does Santa Claus come to your house? Why or why not?
- Nicholas' "Life" was written to inspire others to do good works. Are there people in your life who inspire you to do what is right?
- Does your Christmas resemble Christmas in the Oklahoma Territory in any way?
- Do you buy all of your Christmas gifts, or do you make any of them?

24 Ways to Show Love at Christmas

1. Invite a friend to church
2. Visit someone who may be lonely
3. Donate your time, or a bag of food, to your local soup kitchen or food pantry
4. Bake cookies to give to your neighbors
5. Find out what supplies your local homeless shelter is in need of and donate
6. Mail a book to a child facing a difficult Christmas season
7. Find a charity to volunteer at during the holidays; take a friend with you
8. Give money anonymously to someone in need
9. Cook a meal for a family in difficulty
10. Make Christmas cards and deliver them to residents at a nursing home
11. Take home-baked goods to your police and/or fire station with a thank you card
12. Send a holiday care package to someone
13. Choose to forgive and show love to someone who has hurt your feelings
14. Invite a foreign student to join you for Christmas

15. Volunteer to babysit free of charge for a family with young children
16. Look out for people needing help opening doors, or carrying packages
17. Make a prayer list of people in need of encouragement
18. Make an effort to smile more
19. Volunteer to pet-sit for a neighbor while they are gone over Christmas
20. Thank your teachers for all they do to help you grow and learn
21. Ask a parent if they need extra help; cheerfully do what they request
22. Shovel snow or de-ice a neighbor's sidewalk or driveway
23. Take a bouquet of flowers to someone in need of encouragement
24. Give a small gift card for coffee to someone who least expects it

Christmas Commercialized
Bayside, New York, Christmas Eve, 1957

*C*hildren, *go put on your new Christmas outfits, and Laura, bring me your brush so I can fix your hair. Quickly now! Dad wants to head to church in thirty minutes.*

"Yes Mom," called Laura and Arthur as they ran out of the living room, stopping to furtively grab a piece of peppermint candy from the porcelain snowman in the hall.

A few minutes later, Laura stood patiently while her mother braided her hair. "I've got the ham in the oven, and the spritz cookies, shortbread, and date nut loaves on the table. There are cold salads in the icebox and crackers and cheese on the back porch. Dad is in charge of the drinks. You and Arthur need to be on your best behavior when our guests come." Mrs. Winton put her hand to her forehead and exhaled. "My, but Christmas is a busy time of year!"

An hour later, the family stood in the pew at the local Methodist church, candles in hand, the words of "Silent Night" rising from the mouths of the congregation as the lit candles cast a dreamy glow around them. Snow was falling outside, just enough to make Christmas in the city suburbs beautiful, and provide a pleasing backdrop to the Christmas lights draped on bushes and trees.

Back at home, guests began streaming in the front door for the Winton's annual Christmas Eve open house. Laura watched from behind the couch. She saw their elderly neighbor, Mrs. Mack, arrive, and the new family on the street, the one with two boys Arthur's age. She couldn't wait until her friend, Kathy, came. Kathy was Jewish, and her family celebrated Hanukkah, but they didn't seem to mind attending a Christmas party. A group of Mrs. Winton's friends stood by the tree. Laura and Arthur had hung so much tinsel on the branches that it looked like one of the fake aluminum trees that were so popular this year.

Just then, Laura heard the static from the record player and watched as her dad placed the needle on the shiny black record. Soon the words of "White Christmas" drifted into her ears. She recognized it as the new Christmas song everyone was crazy about. She often caught her mother humming it around the house. Laura had also heard it being played in the department stores when they'd gone into New York City to see the shop window displays on Fifth Avenue. She thought wistfully about those windows: the scenes of mice as large as she was dancing in the snow, or of Sleeping Beauty reclining peacefully in a gilded forest.

"Toot-toot!" "Toot-toot!" Laura looked up with a start. There was Arthur under the tree turning on the trains and making the old ladies smile. There weren't any presents yet, but Laura knew that tomorrow morning the space under the tree would be filled with brightly wrapped packages. She and Arthur would hang their stockings by the fireplace after the party, and they'd leave a glass of milk and a few cookies for Santa. She must remember to bring down the presents she had bought for Mom, Dad, and Arthur. Laura thought about all the trips to the bank with her mom — once a week, beginning in September, they had traipsed past a gigantic cardboard Santa in the foyer of the bank and her mom had deposited ten dollars in the Christmas savings account. On the way home, she'd always given Laura twenty-five cents to put in her own piggy-bank for Christmas shopping in December.

Laura inched her way over to the table of food. She decided on a toothpick stuck with olives, a spoonful of Jello salad, and a buttered roll. She'd come back for cookies later. Aunt Mary beckoned to her from the corner, so she went over to sit next to her.

"Hello, darling. Tell me what you're hoping Santa will bring you for Christmas." Aunt Mary patted Laura's head as Laura settled herself on the rug.

"I'm hoping for Mr. Potato Head and Arthur wants a Pogo Stick."

"A what?" asked Aunt Mary with evident confusion on her face.

"A Pogo Stick — everyone wants one this year, Aunt Mary. It's for jumping around outside."

"Well, what will they think of next," laughed Aunt Mary with a smile.

***

Christmas in the 1950s in America was a time of abundance and joy. The hard years of the Great Depression and World War II were over. Middle class families had enough money to spend on Christmas gifts and decorations. Shops and department stores lined their shelves with every conceivable decoration and gift. Christmas was a booming business, and gifts had become the primary focus of this annual holiday.

Originally, gift-giving had not been a large part of Christmas. Gifts may have been given to children on December 6, St. Nicholas' Day, or exchanged among adults on New Year's Day in centuries past. Now, in the mid-1900s, gift-giving was unquestionably part of Christmas.

The monetary cost of Christmas was growing each year. Banks took advantage

of this and started Christmas Savings programs. Families started paying into their savings account early in the fall, and by Christmas, hopefully, they had enough money for their Christmas purchases.

These Christmas expenses included a tree, lights and decorations, food for a party and for Christmas dinner, presents for family, tips for the mailman, the newspaper boy, and the cleaning help. There might be new holiday outfits for the children, Christmas cards for a long list of friends, and cookies for the neighbors.

Religious observance of Christmas had dwindled over the decades. Few people thought of Advent, the weeks leading up to Christmas, as a time of spiritual preparation. Many might consider attending a Christmas Eve service at a local church. Who could resist the nostalgia of singing Christmas carols in a dimly lit room with candles glowing all around? But, that hour might be the only time during the holiday season when Christ was reflected upon.

Santa Claus continued to grow in popularity. Department stores hired men to dress up as Santa and pose with children in order to attract

101

more shoppers. Songs like "Rudolph the Red-Nosed Reindeer" were written and instantly became hits. Books, ornaments, decorations, music, and movies about Santa Claus flooded the market. Santa had, in many ways, replaced Baby Jesus as the focus of Christmas.

The invention of radio, and then television, fueled the demand for Christmas music and Christmas movies. Christmas hymns had given way to Christmas carols, and these had morphed into secular pop songs like: "White Christmas," "Sleigh Ride," "Winter Wonderland," and "Frosty the Snowman." Television provided family entertainment, and slowly the idea of gathering around the TV to watch a movie on Christmas became a tradition. "A Christmas Carol" and "It's a Wonderful Life," were two Christmas movies released during this era that television stations re-air year after year.

Christmas celebrations in America had become so common, and so widespread, that certain minority groups began to feel the pressure to join in. One such group, those of Jewish lineage, felt this struggle deeply. All around them, Americans were celebrating what they deemed to be a very Christian holiday because it had developed around the birth of Christ. Jewish children didn't want to miss out on all the fun of presents, games, and food which their friends were enjoying. Jewish parents didn't want to compromise their own religion. Hanukkah celebrations answered this dilemma and became very popular.

Hanukkah, also known as the Feast of Lights, is the Jewish celebration of the rededication of the Temple in Jerusalem several hundred years before Christ's birth. It is a time for feasting, getting together with family, and exchanging gifts. By promoting Hanukkah, Jews were able to stay true to their religion but also join in with the mid-winter festivities taking place all around them.

Food, as always, played a large role in Christmas celebrations. Modern kitchens, with refrigerators, electric stoves, and even electric mixers made food preparation easier than in previous ages. Canned vegetables and cream soups featured heavily in modern recipes, as did frozen foods. Roast turkey still reigned supreme as the Christmas meat of choice, but ham might be chosen, or roast beef. Side dishes included scalloped potatoes, mashed sweet

 102

potatoes, stuffing, creamed vegetables, a green salad, or a new-fangled Jell-O salad. Pumpkin or mincemeat pie might be served for dessert, and of course the pantry would be laden with all manner of Christmas cookies and candies.

There were many Americans who could not afford a Christmas like this. These Americans either did without, celebrated with little fuss, or were the recipients of gifts through organizations such as "The Christmas Bureau." Toy and food drives were held during the Christmas season to collect gifts and food for families in need. The Salvation Army began it's red kettle collections in the 1890s, raising money throughout the Christmas season to supply families in need with food and other necessities. Giving to those less fortunate remained an important value of the Christmas season.

Christmas had now come through nearly 2,000 years of history. Much of the groundwork for the traditions and practices we experience today had been laid. What remained to be seen was how the Age of Technology would influence the celebration of Christmas.

Suggested Reading
I John 4:9-12; Luke 3:10-11

Discussion Questions

- What was your grandparents' childhood Christmas like?
- Do you see similarities between a 1950s Christmas and your own?
- Do you save up money to buy Christmas presents for others?
- Have you ever donated to an organization raising money to give Christmas presents to those who need them?
- Do you know someone who celebrates Hanukkah?
- What are your favorite Christmas songs?
- Have you ever watched *It's a Wonderful Life* or *A Christmas Carol*?

Vintage Christmas Cookies

Christmas baking in 1950s America was an expression of post-war food abundance, the wider availability of exciting new baking ingredients like chocolate chips, and the time many women had to spend in their kitchens creating food for the holidays. These Candy Cane Cookies will help you "taste" what a vintage Christmas was like. As you enjoy their flavor, consider the downside to the rise of materialism and how that can affect people spiritually.

Candy Cane Cookies

Ingredients:

- 1 cup/128g confectioners/icing sugar
- 1 cup/113g butter (softened)
- 1 egg
- 1 tsp. vanilla
- 1 tsp. peppermint extract
- 3 ½ cups/450g all-purpose flour (plain)
- 1 tsp. baking powder
- ½ tsp. salt
- ½ cup/125ml milk
- ¼ tsp. red food color (coloring paste is best)
- 8 candy canes, crushed

Method:

In the bowl of a stand mixer, beat together confectioner's sugar and softened butter. Add egg and beat again. Mix in vanilla and peppermint extract. In a separate bowl, mix flour, baking powder, and salt. Add the flour mixture to the butter mixture along with the milk and mix until a soft dough comes together. Divide dough in half. Color one half with the red food coloring. Refrigerate doughs for at least one hour. Preheat oven to 350F/180C/160C Fan. Roll long ropes about 1/3 in/1cm thick of each color dough on a lightly floured surface. Cut lengths of dough about four-inches/10cm long. Twist one red and one white rope segment together and form into a candy cane shape.

Place on a parchment paper lined baking sheet. Bake cookies 9-12 minutes until set but not brown. As soon as cookies are removed from oven, sprinkle with crushed candy canes. Place cookies on rack to cool. Makes 36 large cookies.

Christmas Today
London, United Kingdom

Mrs. Dickson called her class to attention with a clap of her hands. "Today we are going to do something a little different!" She motioned for Yuto to come to the front of the room. "We're taking a break from our geography studies today to talk about Christmas celebrations around the world. I've asked Yuto to come up and tell us what he'll be doing for Christmas when he flies back to Japan next week."

Yuto stepped to the front of the classroom and smiled shyly. "Christmas is a new holiday for Japan," he said. "My parents never celebrated it when they were growing up. Today we have Christmas trees and lights in our shopping malls just like here in London. My dad works on Christmas because December 25th is not a holiday, but he always comes home with a Christmas cake, and my mom always cooks roasted chicken legs for dinner." There were puzzled looks so Yuto explained, "It's true! Here in London everyone eats turkey, but in Japan we eat chicken legs and the most delicious Christmas cake made of white sponge layers and filled with strawberries and whipped cream." A dreamy look came over Yuto's face as he described the cake. "We also get one present from our parents and one present from our grandparents." With a nervous chuckle Yuto turned to another Japanese Christmas tradition. "My cousin has a girlfriend now," said Yuto, "and Christmas Eve is a big deal for them, like Valentine's Day here. Couples go out for a special dinner and exchange presents." Yuto caught a classmate rolling his eyes and grinned. "People in Japan don't connect Christmas with any religious observance. We just enjoy a day to receive presents and eat cake."

"Thank you, Yuto," said Mrs. Dickson, "We'll have to think of you eating your chicken legs and Christmas cake while we're downing sprouts and mince pies!" The class giggled at the contrast and Mrs. Dickson motioned for Olivia to come forward. "Olivia is going to tell us about Christmas in Australia and what it's like to have Christmas in summertime." Mrs. Dickson nodded toward Olivia who stood with a bulky cardigan wrapped around her.

"I miss the heat right now in this crazy cold weather and I can't wait to get home for Christmas on the beach!" rattled off Olivia in her Australian accent. "When we came to London, I thought it might be fun to have snow for Christmas but now I'm not so sure," Olivia stopped to catch her breath. "Our family always goes to the beach on Christmas, and we stay there until it's time for the evening fireworks. Mum takes our portable barbecue and we grill our Christmas dinner right there on the sand. Mum even brings along a Christmas pudding! We have trees, and lights, and Santa just like here in London, but we don't have this," ended Olivia, flinging her hand to the window and the chilling rain that was beating down on the glass.

"Perhaps we could all benefit from a little time in Australia just about now," laughed Mrs. Dickson. "I wouldn't mind a bit of sunshine! Speaking of sunshine, Mukisa is going to tell us about Christmas in Uganda where, I understand, it is also quite warm." Mukisa's wide grin flashed white as he strode to the front.

"Christmas in Uganda is so wonderful," said Mukisa as he shook his head slowly from left to right. "We look forward to this day all year. It is the happiest day of the year. It is so peaceful and full of joy."

Mukisa's eyes stared longingly out the window as he continued. "My parents buy us all new outfits and take us back to the village to visit our uncles, aunties and grandparents. On Christmas morning my auntie makes us giant mugs of hot tea with bread and butter. We go to church for several hours and on the way home we make a list of all the wonderful foods we will eat: rice, potatoes, cooked bananas, chicken, and goat. Every child will have their very own soda to drink." Mukisa gave a sudden laugh. "I suppose that doesn't sound so special when we can drink soda every day here in London. But it is a very special treat to us in the village. We don't exchange presents and Santa Claus does not come to us, but we really have the happiest day." Mrs. Dickson smiled at Mukisa's happy memories and

waited until he was seated before calling on Valentina.

"Valentina is going to tell us about Russian Christmas celebrations," explained Mrs. Dickson as she took her seat and waited for Valentina to begin.

"On December 25th," began Valentina, "We do nothing." Valentina swept the air with her hands and paused dramatically, waiting for her words to take effect. "Nothing for Christmas, that is," she continued when everyone looked up. "Our Christmas takes place on January 7th."

Valentina noticed the scrunched brows as her classmates tried to make sense of

that. She attempted to explain, "It all has to do with differences in the Julian and Gregorian calendars. Most of the world uses the Gregorian calendar now, but we all used to use the Julian calendar hundreds of years ago, and when Christmas began it was with the Julian calendar, so that's what we stick with."

Valentina paused again, wondering if she had successfully explained the date or merely confused everyone. "Anyway, we have our Christmas celebration on January 7th. By then we've already had a New Year's celebration on January 1st and exchanged gifts with everyone. During communism, Christmas celebrations were outlawed. Can you imagine?"

Valentina frowned and shook her head, trying to imagine how people tolerated that. "Now we have Christmas trees, and lights, and the shops are decorated and filled with gifts to buy. Our family goes to church on Christmas Eve at midnight, and my mother even follows the forty days of fasting that lead up to Christmas in the Russian Orthodox Church tradition. We often have my grandparents over for roast chicken on Christmas Day."

Valentina was quiet for a moment as she thought. "I think that's it," she said with a shrug and made her way back to her seat.

"Thank you, Valentina," said Mrs. Dickson, "that was very insightful." Mrs. Dickson glanced down at her lesson plan before looking up and calling Alberto to come forward. "Alberto will tell us about Christmas in Brazil." Mrs. Dickson smiled and indicated for Alberto to begin.

"It is also very hot in my country at Christmas so please come visit!" invited Alberto with enthusiasm. The class clapped in approval. "We have Christmas trees and decorations too, but the nativity scene is Brazil's most traditional decoration. Because it is summer for us in December, we also have lots of fresh flowers. Every Christmas Eve we have a giant feast."

Alberto grinned at the thought. "We have pork, turkey or codfish, and rice with raisins in it, lots of salads, and plenty of nuts. Our family enjoys tropical desserts and there is always more ice cream than any of us can eat. We eat late in the evening, open our presents, and then go immediately to midnight mass at church. Before we can go to bed, there are fireworks! We are so tired on Christmas morning that we sleep in and go to church in the afternoon. Santa Claus comes, but we call him Father Noel."

Alberto paused a moment, considering whether to go on. Mrs. Dickson looked up, but Alberto continued, "You shouldn't tell your parents this, but in Brazil everyone gets a second paycheck in December to help pay for the costs of Christmas!" Alberto laughed at the amazement that spread over the faces in the room. "It's true," said Alberto. "Just come to Brazil and you will see!"

Mrs. Dickson walked to the front of the classroom as Alberto took his seat. "Well, class, we've now heard what it's like to celebrate Christmas in five different countries. Who is willing to describe their British Christmas for the rest of us?"

Mrs. Dickson scanned the hands being raised. "Thomas, you come forward and tell us about your Christmas." Thomas made his way to the front.

"It's certainly not hot in the U.K. at Christmas!" blurted Thomas as he reached the front. The class laughed and shifted in their seats. "In my house

Christmas is a bit hectic. Mum runs around all of December trying to buy a long list of presents for all the relatives we'll be seeing and Dad tries to calm her down. She agonizes for weeks about the 'round robin' letter she insists on writing each year, detailing everything my sister and I have done, and then finally emails it to all her acquaintances." Mrs. Dickson chuckled in the background.

"Mum's always telling us to be good so Santa will be sure to come." Thomas rolled his eyes for effect. "Dad puts lights up on the outside of our house, mostly because all the other neighbors do it too. Our tree is kept in the attic and it's an ordeal to get it down and decorated. Sometimes on Christmas Eve we go to church with Gran. Christmas morning we get up at 6am and rush downstairs to open our stockings and presents. The last two years, our family has signed up for the Santa Fun Run on Christmas morning. After we open presents we all change into red Santa suits and go run a 5k for charity. My sister complains, but I think it's hilarious fun. We go to our Gran's for Christmas Dinner and we always listen to the Queen's speech before we tuck in. Gran cooks a turkey with the sage and onion stuffing, sprouts, parsnips, roast potatoes, and bread sauce."

Thomas stopped for breath and rushed on, "Of course there's the Christmas pud and maybe a chocolate gateau for us children too. After dinner, Dad turns the telly on and I join my friends online to play games. We're so tired when we get home from Gran's, but then we remember we're doing it all over again tomorrow, Boxing Day, with Dad's side of the family."

"Thank you, Thomas," Mrs. Dickson called after Thomas as he took his seat. "It has been fascinating hearing about each of your Christmas experiences and traditions." The students heard the bell in the hallway and began rushing to grab their papers as Mrs. Dickson called after them, "Happy Christmas to you all!"

***

Christmas is now a celebration with two thousand years of history behind it. From a simple commemoration of the birth of Jesus Christ, to the biggest holiday observance in the world, Christmas has developed and changed with each new

111

cultural development, religious concern, or technological discovery. Christmas in our modern world, as with Christmas in times past, has both blessing and hardship for those who choose to celebrate it.

A modern Christmas enjoys the blessings of technology and invention: families separated by great distances can still enjoy each other's company through Internet chats or a phone call. Instead of hunting in the forest for a Yule log, one can just turn on the Yule Log on Demand channel on your TV or YouTube. Electricity, pre-made food, and even restaurants make holiday dining a completely different experience than it used to be. Globalization means Christmas traditions are spreading from one side of the world to the other as people travel and work in different countries and bring their traditions with them. Online shopping and the internet make Christmas presents, decorations, and experiences available to anyone with money to spend and an address for delivery.

Christmas is still a wonderful distraction from the hardship of winter in the northern hemisphere. Modern conveniences like central heating, electric lighting, and heated vehicles make winter easier to endure than it used to be. Nevertheless, many people are thankful for a festive season to take their minds off the cold weather, and look forward to time with family and friends.

Christmas in the modern world has become known as a time to promote peace among different cultures and races. Sadly, this "peace" is often not understood as originating in Christ. Nonetheless, efforts to promote peace show the effects of the spread of the gospel and can be celebrated by Christians. Christmastime is also a season when many people who are hostile to the gospel will tolerate the mention of Christ or the story of his birth. This tolerance is another reason for Christians to rejoice, as well as a motivation to continue to share the love of God with others.

As with Christmases in times past, the modern Christmas has its downfalls. High expectations raised by secular culture contribute to overwhelming stress as people seek to create a "perfect Christmas." Many choose to go into debt to meet these expectations. Stores lure people to spend more money than they have. It is hard to act with self-control and contentment when everything around us urges us to spend and indulge.

As a holiday about God's gift to the world, the remembrance of Christ's birth is a possibility for anyone. It doesn't cost money to contemplate the joys of God sending his Son to earth to save us from our sins. Going to church is free. Worshiping our Savior, the Lord Jesus, is an opportunity that many people in this world have available to them. In many very poor countries around the world Christmas remains only a spiritually-focused holiday.

As a holiday about our gifts to one another, Christmas has become something accessible mainly to people with money rather than those who suffer under the heavy burden of poverty. We don't hear about fancy decorations and piles of gifts filling the houses of most families in sub-Saharan Africa or parts of Asia where people make less than $1,000 a year. A fancy Christmas is unthinkable for most of the world's population. As we take part in our cultural celebrations at Christmas, it is helpful to keep in mind that what we are doing is a privilege.

Having money to spend on Christmas is a luxury. As we enjoy these good gifts God has kindly given us, we would do well to consider the plight of those in other, poorer, countries. Setting a limit for our indulgences at Christmas could help us set aside more for giving to those in need. After all, Christmas is the traditional 'birthday' of Jesus, and on birthdays, we give presents to the person whose birthday we are celebrating. Jesus said, 'Truly, I say to you, as you did it to one of the least of these my brothers, you did it to me.' (Matthew 25:40). We can express our love for Jesus, and praise for his Incarnation, by making generosity to the needy a centerpiece of our modern Christmas.

Christmas today might look different than many years ago, but we still face the same challenges as those celebrants of old. The faithful in ages past endeavored to guard Christmas from overindulgence in order to keep the holiday focused on the beauty of the Lord. Christmas has different stresses today, but we continue the same endeavor to focus on Christ in the midst of the materialism of the twenty-first century. May we carry this great heritage into the future with Christmas celebrations that point to Christ and the beautiful story of redemption!

Suggested Reading

Ephesians 4:1-6; Gal 5:22-23;
Hebrews 13:15-16

Discussion Questions

- What are your country's Christmas traditions?

- Do you have friends who celebrate Christmas differently than you do?

- What technologies do you make use of at Christmastime?

- Does your family feel rushed during the holiday season? If so, how could you slow down?

- What are some ways you could love your neighbors, or people you see regularly, at Christmastime?

- What do you think Christmas will be like in the future?

- What helps you to remember how much God loves you?

24 Ways to Enjoy a Modern Christmas

1. Visit a tree farm and cut your own Christmas tree
2. Buy a chocolate-filled Advent calendar
3. Buy, rather than bake, Christmas treats
4. Attend church
5. Find a Holiday Yule Log channel to play on your TV
6. Use battery-operated candles to decorate
7. Participate in a charity race
8. Watch Santa's "progress" on NORAD
9. Donate to charities online
10. Go to an outdoor Christmas light display
11. Buy matching Christmas pajamas for the family
12. Attend a school concert
13. Participate in a "Secret Santa" exchange
14. Send Christmas greetings via email or text
15. Host a "White Elephant" gift exchange
16. Go ice skating at an outdoor rink
17. Enjoy a video chat with far away relatives
18. Take your live Christmas tree to be recycled after Christmas
19. Go to the theatre to see a movie
20. Wear an "ugly Christmas sweater"
21. Spend Christmas Eve volunteering at a local charity
22. Visit an open-air Christmas market
23. Go to a Christmas parade
24. Open presents on Christmas Day rather than Christmas Eve

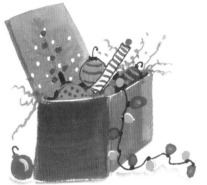

What's Next for Christmas?

Here we are with 2000 years of Christmas history behind us — a history rich in meaning, symbolism, and tradition, yet sometimes fraught with disagreement and division. Christmas, like life, is complicated. And it can be even more complicated for Christians: what to celebrate, how to celebrate, should we celebrate?

As we have seen in this book, Christmas has been observed in different ways in various periods and places around the world. Perhaps the most distinctive feature of Christmas celebrations today, is that there is no single set of customs to be followed. As the world grows more connected, the ways of celebrating Christmas seem to be increasingly diverse. Even within the Church, Christians have a variety of traditions and convictions regarding Christmas.

Your family may enjoy celebrating a long and full Christmas season complete with decorations, presents, church services, visits to Santa, and an overwhelming calendar of social gatherings. Perhaps you know a friend who has chosen not to include Santa Claus in their celebrations. You may even have Christian friends who do not celebrate Christmas at all, but remember the Incarnation in other ways. The Apostle Paul urges us to respect one another and be united by our joy in the work of Christ, despite differing practices for celebrating his salvation (see Romans 14:5-6). If there is one lesson that the history of Christmas shows us, it is the timeless and cross-cultural impact of such a great salvation as revealed in the manger.

The fact that Christmas has eclipsed so many other holidays around the world, to become a virtually universal celebration of peace and love, is a testimony to the gripping truth that God so loved the world, he came to us as a helpless infant. The Creator of the universe has so loved this dark, cold, and suffering world, that he came to dwell among us—not in the halls of the great, but entering our world in the hovels of the poor. Nothing has gripped the hearts and imaginations of men, women, and children across races, languages, times, and traditions quite like that powerful event.

The traditions of Christmas have changed through history. But it is the marvel of the Incarnation that remains, and must be upheld as, the centerpiece

of our celebration. The Incarnation is the theological term Christians use to describe Christ taking on the body of a human and being born here on earth. Emmanuel, meaning God with us, is the name we call Christ because of his Incarnation. Taking time to ponder that God could love us to such an extent, that he chose to dwell with us here on earth, is one way Christmas can draw us closer to Christ each year.

As we grow in our understanding of the richness of God's love for us, a natural result will be wanting to show God's love to others. The Bible teaches us that our love for God is directly related to how much we love others (1 John). Christmastime should remind us yet again that we, as Christians, ought to be about the daily work of loving others.

Christmas provides many opportunities to show love: sending cards and gifts to those in need, visiting the lonely, inviting those far from home to celebrate with you, or simply performing mundane chores with love and joy.

One thing we can learn from the Incarnation is that God deeply desires to have fellowship with us. We can enjoy this fellowship in worship services, in prayer, and in times of Bible reading.

Christmas is an opportune time of year for drawing into closer fellowship with God and seeking for ways to have fellowship with others. Inviting others for meals, attending church, spending time together as a family, asking a store clerk how they are doing, or reaching out to people are just a few ideas of ways to encourage fellowship with others.

As Christians, our thoughts and actions should be filled with the knowledge of God's love for us and our love for others each and every day of the year, not just at Christmas. Sadly, because we are imperfect, we forget God's love too easily, and often neglect to show love to others. Let Christmas remind us of what is most important, and spur us on yet again to love and good works.

So what is next for Christmas? Where does it go from here? Will it lose popularity in a few hundred years and cease to be? Will it become so expensive and overwhelming that people give up its remembrance? Will there come a time when the birth of Christ is no longer connected with the cultural aspects of Christmas? Could children learn to expect less and give more and still have a happy Christmas? Would it be possible for Christians to cherish the Incarnation in a deeper way all year long? Could a deeper understanding of God's love for us have a lasting impact on the world around us?

Through much of history, various forces have influenced the changing traditions of Christmas. Sometimes, business interests have pressed Christmas celebration into more consumer-focused directions. Political or social pressures have endeavored to restrain or expand the indulgences associated with the season. What the Church has done is point our hearts back to Christ. Christians in the present day should do the same.

With the knowledge of how Christmas has been celebrated in the past, and our own experience of Christmas in the present, it is our responsibility to lay foundations for the future history of Christmas in the traditions we pass along in our homes and churches.

The choices and decisions we make today will shape this holiday for our children and grandchildren. As Christians, we can choose to let Christmas communicate to others the joy, peace, and love contained in the gospel, abiding in God's love for us and seeking to share that love with others.

History of Christmas Timeline

THE BIRTH OF CHRIST
6 BC - approximate Birth of Christ

EARLY CHURCH
64	Nero persecutes Christians in Rome
313	Edict of Milan: Christianity legalized in the Roman Empire
345	December 25 declared Christ's birthdate by Pope Julius I
476	Fall of the Roman Empire
570	Mohammed, founder of Islam, born
725	Boniface spreads Christianity in what would become Germany
800	Charlemagne crowned Holy Roman Emperor
1038	Christmas referred to as "Cristes maesse"
1054	The Church divides into the Eastern Orthodox and the Roman Catholic churches
1066	Battle of Hastings
1066	William the Conqueror crowned king on Christmas Day
1096	The Crusades begin
1215	The Magna Carta is signed in England
1223	Francis of Assisi creates the first live nativity

1347   Black Death in Europe begins
1381   Wycliffe begins to translate the Bible into English
1440   Johannes Gutenberg invents the printing press
1492   Columbus lands in the Caribbean

REFORMERS AND PURITANS
1517   Martin Luther nails his 95 Theses on the door in Wittenberg (October 31)
1534   England breaks away from the Roman Catholic Church
1611   King James Version of the Bible published
1620   The Pilgrims land at Plymouth in the New World
1642   Civil War in England
1644   The English Parliament cancels Christmas and calls for a day of fasting
1741   George Fredrick Handel composes "The Messiah"
1774   Christmas in Williamsburg
1776   Declaration of Independence in America
1793   William Carey becomes the first British missionary, travels to India

VICTORIANS TO MODERN DAY
1837   Queen Victoria ascends British throne
1850   Christmas with Charles Dickens and family
1861   American Civil War begins
1865   American Civil War ends
1865   Hudson Taylor founds the China Inland Mission
1886   Gasoline automobile invented
1896   Christmas in the Oklahoma Territory
1914   World War One begins
1918   World War One ends
1939   World War Two begins
1945   World War Two ends
1953   IBM introduces its first commercial computer
1957   Christmas in an age of commercialization
1975   Vietnam War ends
1991   Fall of the Soviet Union
2019   Christmas today

Luke 2
The Birth of Jesus Christ (ESV)

In those days a decree went out from Caesar Augustus that all the world should be registered. ² This was the first registration when Quirinius was governor of Syria. ³ And all went to be registered, each to his own town. ⁴ And Joseph also went up from Galilee, from the town of Nazareth, to Judea, to the city of David, which is called Bethlehem, because he was of the house and lineage of David, ⁵ to be registered with Mary, his betrothed, who was with child. ⁶ And while they were there, the time came for her to give birth. ⁷ And she gave birth to her firstborn son and wrapped him in swaddling cloths and laid him in a manger, because there was no place for them in the inn.

The Shepherds and the Angels
⁸ And in the same region there were shepherds out in the field, keeping watch over their flock by night. ⁹ And an angel of the Lord appeared to them, and the glory of the Lord shone around them, and they were filled with great fear. ¹⁰ And the angel said to them, "Fear not, for behold, I bring you good news of great joy that will be for all the people. ¹¹ For unto you is born this day in the city of David a Savior, who is Christ the Lord. ¹² And this will be a sign for you: you will find a baby wrapped in swaddling cloths and lying in a manger." ¹³ And suddenly there was with the angel a multitude of the heavenly host praising God and saying,

¹⁴ "Glory to God in the highest,
   and on earth peace among those with whom he is pleased!"

¹⁵ When the angels went away from them into heaven, the shepherds said to one another, "Let us go over to Bethlehem and see this thing that has happened, which the Lord has made known to us." ¹⁶ And they went with haste and found Mary and Joseph, and the baby lying in a manger. ¹⁷ And when they saw it, they made known the saying that had been told them concerning this child. ¹⁸ And all who heard it wondered at what the shepherds told them. ¹⁹ But Mary treasured up all these things, pondering them in her heart. ²⁰ And the shepherds returned, glorifying and praising God for all they had heard and seen, as it had been told them.
²¹ And at the end of eight days, when he was circumcised, he was called Jesus, the name given by the angel before he was conceived in the womb.

Jesus Presented at the Temple

22 And when the time came for their purification according to the Law of Moses, they brought him up to Jerusalem to present him to the Lord 23 (as it is written in the Law of the Lord, "Every male who first opens the womb shall be called holy to the Lord") 24 and to offer a sacrifice according to what is said in the Law of the Lord, "a pair of turtledoves, or two young pigeons." 25 Now there was a man in Jerusalem, whose name was Simeon, and this man was righteous and devout, waiting for the consolation of Israel, and the Holy Spirit was upon him. 26 And it had been revealed to him by the Holy Spirit that he would not see death before he had seen the Lord's Christ. 27 And he came in the Spirit into the temple, and when the parents brought in the child Jesus, to do for him according to the custom of the Law, 28 he took him up in his arms and blessed God and said,

29 "Lord, now you are letting your servant depart in peace, according to your word;
30 for my eyes have seen your salvation
31 that you have prepared in the presence of all peoples,
32 a light for revelation to the Gentiles,
 and for glory to your people Israel."

33 And his father and his mother marveled at what was said about him. 34 And Simeon blessed them and said to Mary his mother, "Behold, this child is appointed for the fall and rising of many in Israel, and for a sign that is opposed 35 (and a sword will pierce through your own soul also), so that thoughts from many hearts may be revealed."

36 And there was a prophetess, Anna, the daughter of Phanuel, of the tribe of Asher. She was advanced in years, having lived with her husband seven years from when she was a virgin, 37 and then as a widow until she was eighty-four. She did not depart from the temple, worshiping with fasting and prayer night and day. 38 And coming up at that very hour she began to give thanks to God and to speak of him to all who were waiting for the redemption of Jerusalem.

The Return to Nazareth

39 And when they had performed everything according to the Law of the Lord, they returned into Galilee, to their own town of Nazareth. 40 And the child grew and became strong, filled with wisdom. And the favor of God was upon him.

Christian Focus Publications

Christian Focus Publications publishes books for adults and children under its four main imprints: Christian Focus, CF4K, Mentor and Christian Heritage. Our books reflect our conviction that God's Word is reliable and Jesus is the way to know him, and live for ever with him. Our children's list includes a Sunday School curriculum that covers pre-school to early teens, and puzzle and activity books. We also publish personal and family devotional titles, biographies and inspirational stories that children will love. If you are looking for quality Bible teaching for children, then we have an excellent range of Bible stories and age-specific theological books. From pre-school board books to teenage apologetics, we have it covered!